A Worcestershire Dynasty

By the same Author:
Worcestershire Salt,
A History of Stoke Prior Salt Works

To my dear wife Fran.

A Worcestershire Dynasty

Dixons of Tardebigge
The History of a
North Worcestershire
Family Farming and Business Empire

by

The Revd. Alan White, M.Sc, M.A., M.Ed.

Priest in Charge of the Parish of Tardebigge

Brewin Books

First published December 1997

by Brewin Books, Studley, Warwickshire.

ISBN 1 85858 110 9

British Library Cataloguing in Publication Data
A Catalogue record for this book is available
from the British Library

Typeset in Palatino
and made and printed by
Heron Press, Kings Norton, Birmingham

Contents

List of Illustrations

Introduction

For a great many years the firm of T & M Dixon was a large business empire centred in the northern part of the Parish of Tardebigge, between Bromsgrove and Redditch, in north-east Worcestershire. It all began when Thomas Dixon, a canal carrier and coal dealer in Birmingham, came out to Tardebigge Old Wharf in 1809, rented the Lower House, Stoney Lane, and began to farm locally. Eventually two of his grandsons, Thomas and Matthew, developed the business in partnership as T & M Dixon. They widened its horizons and eventually it included, besides coal and farm produce distributed and sold widely, also lime, timber, hard and soft fruit, and garages in Redditch. The history of the family and of the growth and development of the business and its eventual decline and disintegration following World War 2, is a fascinating one.

In researching the overall history of the family business I have received special help from several interested relatives of the family. One of these, Timothy (Tiger) Dixon, is a great grandson of Matthew Dixon. His father, Ernald Dixon, worked for some time in Dixons' Redditch office. Tiger has kindly supplied much information and also photographs of the early members of the family, Thomas and Rebecca Dixon, Thomas and Mary Dixon, and the Thomas and Matthew of the business partnership. Harry Thompson, another great grandson of Matthew, and his wife Ann have also generously provided family details and have made available various documents and photographs. Mrs Margaret Benton, sister of the late Dudley Thompson, kindly sent me a copy of "Tardebigge in the 1920s" which forms part of a comprehensive Dixon family history which he spent much time researching and compiling, and I am grateful to Dudley's daughter Mrs Lynda Brown, one of his executors, for permission to include it as a chapter in this book. From Colonel Matthew Dixon, brother of Crispian and Peter Dixon, I have received several photographs for which I am also grateful.

I was fortunate, a few years ago, to be able to visit and talk to the late Jack Houghton who worked as clerk and secretary for T & M Dixon and latterly for Tardebigge Orchards for altogether sixty years from 1911 to 1971. I like to think that my interest in what he was able to tell me encouraged him to compile his typescript memoirs "I Remember - My first 90 years 1/10/1897 to 1/10/1987". From these memoirs, I have extracted those sections which relate to his life and work for Dixons and which throw much light upon the way the business was run. I am grateful to Jack's daughter, Alison Houghton, for allowing me the use of his memoirs and for the photograph of her father outside the Broad Green offices of T & M Dixon.

There are many people still living who were employed by T & M Dixon and who can remember various aspects of the farming and other business activities which dominated the life of the locality and served the needs of people far and wide. Some of them have supplied first hand information about their work and have contributed to the overall picture of the extensive operation, especially at its peak in the 1920s and 1930s. Their reminiscences and those of other people are included in chapter 4 and I am grateful to all who kindly supplied them.

A number of other persons have also helped in the piecing together of the history. Ian Hayes, a local historian, during his researches found the plan of the extension of the Redditch Railway showing the Hewell Road coal wharf which was then occupied by T & M Dixon. Mrs Winifred Bird collaborated with her husband John Bird in getting the facts right about the final years of T & M Dixon (Farmers) and the formation and fortunes of Tardebigge Orchards which followed on. I am very grateful for their interest and their generous help.

Other sources of information have included the files of local newspapers in the Bromsgrove and Redditch public libraries, parish records and census records held on film in the County Records Office at Worcester, and minutes of the committee of the Worcester and Birmingham Canal Company held in the National Records Office at Kew.

Alan White
October 1997.

Chapter One
A History of the Family Business

Beginnings at Birmingham and Tardebigge

On Monday 30 March 1807 the Worcester and Birmingham Canal, then under construction, was opened from Birmingham as far as Tardebigge Old Wharf. In the previous August the Canal Company had advertised in the Birmingham and Worcester newspapers inviting potential carriers of coal from the Wharf to Redditch, Alcester, Evesham etc. to submit tenders for carriage per ton and also to stipulate what quantities they could carry per week or month. On 6 March 1807 the Canal Committee allotted boat lengths for loading and unloading at the Wharf, together with a stacking ground adjacent to each length, to six applicants, one being Thomas Dixon & Co. of Birmingham. On later bill headings of T & M Dixon it was stated that the business had been established in 1790, but little is known of its beginnings. However, we do know something of the family history of Thomas Dixon, its founder. He was born in 1756 and married Rebecca Tilley of Rowley Regis in 1776. Thomas and Rebecca had three sons. The eldest, Matthew, was born in 1777; the others, Thomas and William, twins, were born in 1779.

Whatever his previous employment had been, Thomas evidently started up in a carrying and coal business with his own boat in 1790, probably in the Black Country on the Birmingham or the Dudley Canal. Assisted by his sons, his business had prospered to the point where, in 1807, he was able to take over that of Henry Weeks who became bankrupt early that year. Weeks was a London carrier who, from 1803, had occupied a wharf alongside the Birmingham Canal just off Broad Street, then on the western outskirts of Birmingham town. From this wharf on the west side of the Canal as it curved round towards Bridge Street to enter its terminus at the Old Wharf, Thomas Dixon managed his own canal carrying business to and from London and other destinations, until he moved to Tardebigge.

A few months after the Wharf opened at Tardebigge, a firm of carriers, Cresswell and Co., who did not have their own boat length there, were advertising for business to carry goods, using the Worcester and Birmingham Canal from Birmingham to Tardebigge, land carriage from there to Droitwich, and then the Droitwich Barge Canal and River

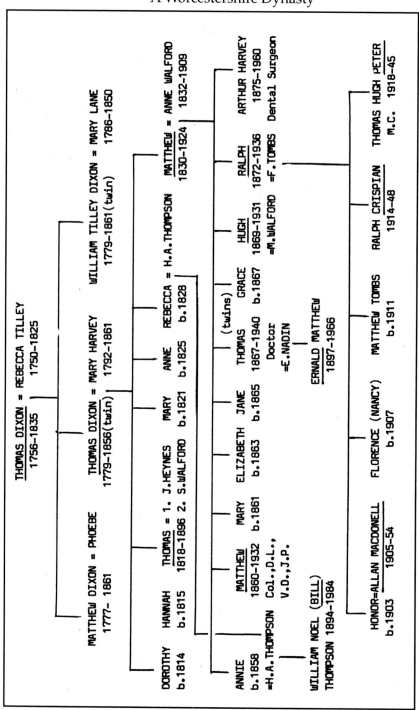

Five generations of the Dixon family tree, with those involved in the family business underlined.

Severn to Worcester and Bristol. Cresswell & Co. had a wharf in Droitwich as well as a wharf and warehouse in Worcester for their coal trade. On 26 May 1808 another advertisement appeared in Berrow's Worcester Journal from Messrs. Cresswell and Barnes, advertising for business and mentioning "T.Dixon & Co. with whom they have now formed a connection in order to remedy the complaints of several of their friends". At that time Cresswells were evidently using T.Dixon & Company's boats to expedite the carriage of their goods as far as Tardebigge.

Cresswell and Barnes' arrangement with Thomas Dixon did not last long, for the connection was terminated on 1 April 1909 and the following advertisement appeared in Berrow's Worcester Journal of 13 April 1809:-

Severn Wharf, Birmingham.

Thomas Dixon & Co., London and Bristol Carriers, respectfully inform the Mercantile Interest and the Trade in general of Worcester, Bristol, Birmingham, etc. that the connection which existed between themselves and Messrs. Cresswell and Barnes in the carrying trade terminated on the 1st. day of April inst.

Thomas Dixon & Co. avail themselves of the present occasion to return their most grateful acknowledgements to their numerous friends for the liberal and unprecedented encouragement they have experienced since their commencement in the carrying trade and to solicit a continuance of these favours it is their desire to merit.

Consignments made to Mr. John Holt, Axe Inn, Aldermanbury, London; Mr. John White, Gloucester; the Packhorse Inn, Worcester or the Severn Wharf, Birmingham, will meet due attention.

Their Waggons meet their Boats at Tardebigge and convey goods direct to Worcester. The same Waggons return with goods to Tardebigge where they have Boats waiting. In short they have adapted such general arrangements for facilitating the expeditious conveyance of goods upon the Birmingham and Worcester Canal and the River Severn to Gloucester, Bristol and all parts of the West of England that they make no doubt will insure them the future favours of their friends. N.B. The Connection above alluded to was not a Partnership.

Birmingham. April 7, 1809.

By this time, T.Dixon & Co., which included Thomas Dixon senior and his three sons and was based at the Severn Wharf in Birmingham, was well established and business was increasing at Tardebigge. On 26 April 1809, following the termination of the "connection" between them, the Canal Committee ordered "Messrs. Dixon and Cresswell to have joint use of the warehouse at Tardebigge, one to take the right hand side, and the other the left, and that Mr. Dixon have the choice of sides." One wonders whether, or for how long, the two firms were able to coexist at Tardebigge after their severance.

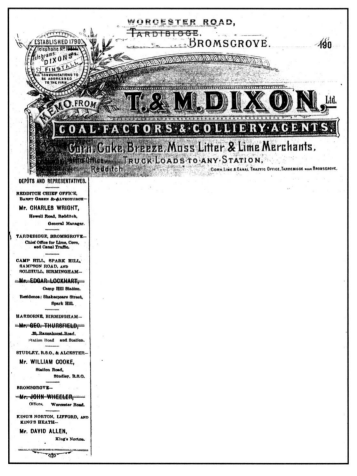

T & M Dixon Limited billhead, early twentieth century, with date of establishment and list of depots for coal etc.

The Move to Tardebigge

In 1808 the Lower House, Stoney Lane, with surrounding farmland and located only a few hundred yards from the Wharf at Tardebigge, came up for auction and was bought by the Plymouth Estates which already owned most of the land thereabouts. The tenancy of the Lower House was available and Thomas Dixon seized the opportunity to make his home there, in pleasant rural surroundings away from industrial Birmingham, with an eye to farming and the carriage of farm produce to Birmingham on his boats. An added attraction may have been the Canal Company's decision that from May 1807 farmers who bought coal from the wharf at Tardebigge were allowed carriage, free of charge, on wheat, barley, oats, beans, peas, flour, meal, malt and bran on boats returning to Birmingham. The lease of the Lower House, with 77 acres of farm land adjoining the canal, from the Earl of Plymouth to Thomas Dixon and his two sons Thomas and William, was dated July 22nd. 1810. By this time Thomas and Rebecca and son Thomas were living in the Lower House. William, who also came out from Birmingham about the same time, was living with his wife at Horns Hall Farm, on the opposite side of Stoney Lane, not far from the Lower House. The eldest son Matthew, who was also married, remained in Birmingham and lived in Hunters Lane, Aston.

The Runaway Marriage of Son Thomas and Mary Harvey

In 1809 William had married Mary Lane of Rous Lench near Evesham (he might have met her whilst delivering coal in that area) and their two eldest children, Mary Lane Dixon and Helen Maria Dixon were baptised in 1811 and 1813 at St. Bartholomew's Church, Tardebigge. By 1815, however, William had fallen out with his father and twin brother and he and his family returned that year to live in Birmingham. While they were still living at Horns Hall, in February 1813, William and Mary Dixon invited a girl friend of Mary's to stay with them. The guest was 21-year-old Mary Harvey of Weethley near Alcester, and she was very much in love with William's twin brother Thomas Dixon, aged 33. It seems that Mary and Thomas were already acquainted, for Mary's widowed mother was a coal customer of the Dixons, as we know from surviving weighbridge bills of 1810 at the Old Wharf and 1816 at the New Wharf. Without telling Mary's mother and

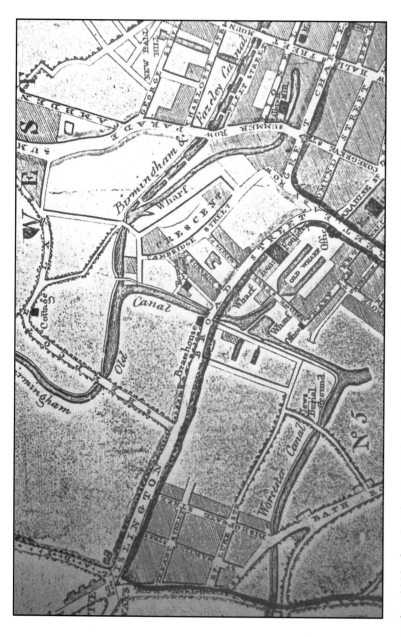

Map circa 1810, showing the Birmingham Canals. Until the Worcester and Birmingham Canal was completed to Worcester in 1815 it had been separated from the old Birmingham Canal near broad Street by a watertight 7ft wide strip of land called the Worcester Bar. Dixon and Co. operated both from the Old Wharf of the Birmingham Canal and from the Worcester Wharf on the Worcester and Birmingham Canal.

family the couple slipped off to Birmingham where they were married in Aston Church, probably from Thomas's brother Matthew's house, on 1st.March 1813. It may have been this run-away marriage which caused the rift between the twin brothers, but, whether or not this was the case, it immediately caused a terrible storm in other quarters.

On the day of the wedding, the bride's widowed mother wrote to her daughter to enquire why she had not returned home from her three-week stay. The newly-weds received the letter two days later on their return to Stoney Lane and both replied on 4th. March to break the news of their marriage. Thomas wrote: "Honored Madam, I feel it is a painful duty to address you at the present time because I know not in what manner you will receive the information of my marriage to your daughter Mary - she might perhaps have married a man in greater affluence but I have the pleasure to say that I have a sufficiency to keep her in a respectable manner and that I love and admire her above all other women on earth and have every reason to believe our affection is mutual - the confidence of which induced me to embrace the first opportunity of making her my own and I thank God I have accomplished it." Mary also wrote an apologetic letter from which it appears that her mother already had a dim view of Thomas and would have disapproved of her marriage: "My Dear Mother, I received your kind letter on the 3rd. and am sorry that I prevented your going to Mr. Ruffords by my not coming home but I trust when you know the reason your goodness will forgive me as I have been for some time endeavouring to please you and myself; I find it quite impossible to do both, therefore I have now married a man whom I am quite convinced will make a good husband and I have every reason to think that when we come to Weethley and you have had a conversation with him you will be very much pleased with his goodness of heart though his disposition has been misrepresented to you before."

Mrs Harvey was extremely upset and angry at the news of her daughter's marriage, although she was of age, to a much older man whom she clearly believed was below her daughter's station and was after her money and inheritance. A long and acrimonious correspondence (which has survived) ensued between mother and daughter in which the mother reproves her daughter as "an ungrateful girl" and "an undutiful child" and continually refuses to receive her son-in-law into her house, while the daughter with equal insistence refuses to visit her family unless she can do so in company with her husband. This situation continued for over a year, by which time Mary was pregnant, the storm began to subside and there was a reconciliation. In the meanwhile, as remaining weighbridge bills reveal, Mrs Harvey made a point of transferring her coal custom away from Dixon & Co. to Jenkins and Wright on Tardebigge New Wharf and this lasted from 20 March 1813 and throughout 1814.

The marriage of Thomas and Mary seems to have been a happy and fruitful one. They continued to live together at Stoney Lane for many years and raised a family of seven children including the Thomas and Matthew of the later successful partnership of T & M Dixon.

Early Years at the Lower House Farm

For the Dixons, setting up and expanding their business at Tardebigge in the early years seems to have been a struggle. It could not have been easy to find the capital for extra boats, wagons and horses for an expanding carrying business and, at the same time, livestock and equipment for the farming side. Between 1809 and 1816 the Canal Committee minutes record some six occasions when T.Dixon & Co. were threatened with legal action unless their three-monthly accounts for rents and tonnages, £165 in 1809 increasing as trade improved to over £300, were paid. However the situation gradually improved. They were agents for the Hewell Estates, for which they supplied coal and from which they shipped timber. By an original agreement between the Canal Company and the Earl of Plymouth who was its first Chairman, goods to and from the Hewell Estates were carried on the canal free of toll, and Dixons benefited from this concession.

Tardebigge Tunnel was completed and Tardebigge New Wharf opened in January 1811. Dixons soon made additional use of the New Wharf for their coal trade. They also set up six lime- burning kilns near the south-west corner of the New Wharf basin, together with two beside the canal winding hole at the Old Wharf. In these kilns limestone, carried along the Canal from quarries at Himbleton and Dunhampstead, was burnt to provide lime for building and agricultural use. As their coal trade gradually expanded, Dixons opened offices and depots at

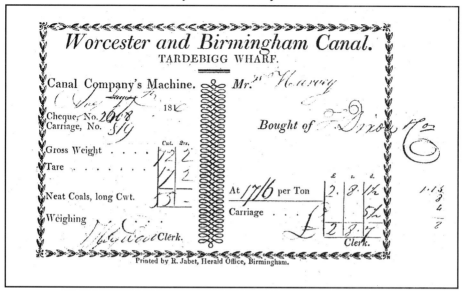

Weighbridge bills for coal supplied by Dixon & Co to Mrs Harvey, at the Old Wharf 1810, at the New Wharf 1816

Kings Norton, Bromsgrove, Redditch and Alcester, besides one already existing in Birmingham. Milk, eggs, poultry and pigs went by canal boat into Birmingham to supply the canalside Queen's Hospital (which later became the Accident Hospital) and other customers. Dixons had their own horses and carts and stables near the Worcester Wharf in Birmingham for the distribution of coal and other goods.

Under The Second Thomas, 1838-56

Thomas Dixon senior was 53 when he and his wife Rebecca came out to Tardebigge in 1809. Rebecca died in 1825 and Thomas died, aged 82, in 1838 and both are buried in Tardebigge Churchyard close to the chancel door. When Thomas senior died, the business was already mainly in the capable hands of his son Thomas, now aged 58, and he was by this time assisted by his own elder son Thomas aged 20. The other six children of Thomas and Mary were all daughters except the youngest, Matthew, then aged 8, who also, in a few years time, joined his father and elder brother in the business. Eventually in 1856, the two sons, Thomas and Matthew, now 38 and 26, lost their father and thereafter they carried on the business in partnership as T & M Dixon.

The T & M Dixon Partnership and Expansion, 1856-1900

For 40 years, from 1856 to 1896 the business partnership of Thomas and Matthew Dixon prospered and extended. The general canal carrying business of the earlier years had given way to the carriage by canal of their own goods, coal, corn and other farm produce mainly, but also timber, limestone, grain for animal feed, waste foodstuffs for pigs and manure for the land. As the years passed, the farming and commercial interests of the Dixon brothers expanded and diversified.

In 1858-59 the branch railway from Barnt Green to Redditch was being constructed and it opened in the Autumn of 1859. The railway then terminated at Hewell Road, Redditch, and the original passenger station was situated on the east side of the track alongside Clive Road (formerly called Station Road). A two-track goods siding was constructed on the west side and the access to the goods yard was from Hewell Road. Three years after the opening of the Redditch Branch, an 1862 plan of the proposed extension of it to Evesham shows T & M Dixon as one of four coal dealers renting coal wharves in the railway goods yard alongside the

The Lower House, Tardebigge, Dixon family home from 1809 to 1937.

sidings from the landowners, the Windsors of Hewell. Dixons' coal wharf, office, weighing machine and machine house were just inside the Hewell Road entrance to the yard, suggesting that they were probably the first enterprising coal merchants to make use of the branch railway for the delivery of coal. From local directories and from Dixons' bills and business notepaper, we know that the Hewell Road Depot was managed by Luke Houghton in the 1870s, and later, around 1900, by Charles Wright. Dixons gradually took over and leased from the Hewell Estate the whole of the railway goods yard and developed there, in addition to their coal business, an extensive timber, building materials and, eventually, a haulage and garage business. They also built up their own fleet of privately-owned railway wagons for the transport of coal and timber.

Besides the development of the Hewell Road site in Redditch, depots and offices were maintained over the years at Studley, Alcester, Bromsgrove, Harborne, Kings Norton, and at Camp Hill and Barnt Green Stations, mainly dealing in coal, but also supplying building materials, animal feeds etc. The old warehouse on the New Wharf at

Tardebigge was rented from the Canal Company and used as a grist mill for the production of animal feeds, a portable steam engine being used to power the machinery. Also at both the New Wharf and the Old Wharf T & M Dixon continued the use of the lime-burning kilns to produce lime for building and agricultural use.

Relations with the Windsor family and the Hewell Estate, of which the Dixons were tenants, remained cordial and mutually beneficial. The House and Estate were supplied by T & M Dixon with coal and coke and they bought timber off the Estate. It is likely that Dixons' boats were involved in the transport of stone and other materials by canal for the building of the new Hewell Grange in the late 1880s. Much of the stone came from quarries at Runcorn in Cheshire; it was unloaded at the Old Wharf, where a crane was installed, and was transported from there by horse-drawn wagons on a temporary tramway. An interesting letter from the Earl of Plymouth, then in Scotland, to Matthew Dixon in September 1911 remarked upon the Dixon family's 100-year tenancy of the Lower House Farm and cordial relationship which had existed over the years: "I count myself very fortunate that this long connection between our families has existed with much confidence and esteem on both sides - I trust that it may long continue. Will you please accept a haunch of venison which I am sending you, shot by Mr. Archer Windsor Clive on Sep. 25th. weighing 17 stone 1 lb."

Unfortunately there is a dearth of surviving records of the business and the many people employed by T & M Dixon during the latter part of the nineteenth century. The acreage farmed by them steadily increased as more land was rented or purchased. Census records show that by 1861 the area farmed had increased from the original 77 acres to 318 acres and that 17 labourers and 4 boys were then employed. By 1871 490 acres were being farmed by 16 labourers and 2 boys, evidently with greater economy and efficiency. Expansion continued until by 1900 the farms covered some 800 acres, well over a square mile of the north-east Worcestershire countryside.

T & M Dixon continued to make good use of the canal, having some fifty of their own canal boats. Most of these were day boats with small cabins, and the crews, if away from home at night, would sleep at Dixons' own stables in Birmingham. Under the Canal Boats Act of 1879, boats with cabins equipped for sleeping and living aboard had to be

registered. Between 1879 and 1900 twelve such boats belonging to
Dixons were registered with the Birmingham Sanitary Authority. They
plied mainly between Tardebigge and Birmingham and collieries at
Cannock and Hednesford, and carried, besides coal, also hay, corn, and
manure, In each case the master of the boat is listed as Thomas
Colledge. He had been appointed by Dixons about 1870 to be in charge
of their fleet of boats, and ten years later he became sub-postmaster at
the post office and shop on Tardebigge New Wharf. He himself could
neither read nor write; it was his wife Mary who ran the business which
was open from 7.00 am to 8.00 pm on weekdays. Thomas Colledge's
father William lived in a small cottage (long demolished) at the Old
Wharf and had probably worked on Dixons' boats before him. Tom
himself, besides being in charge of Dixons' boats and boatmen, also

Thomas and Rebecca Dixon (first generation)

organised deliveries of coal from Cannock and other pits. He had three
sons, John, William (Bill), and George, who worked on the boats in their
younger days. John succeeded his father in charge of Dixons' boats
until about 1920. Bill went to live in Birmingham and, with the help of

his three sons, Eddie, Will and Jack, worked two of Dixons' boats in the Birmingham area. George became a coal merchant at Scarfield Wharf, Alvechurch. When he died in the flu' epidemic following the 1914-18 War, his horse-drawn boat *Snowdrop* was bought and used by Dixons.

Thomas the Senior Partner

Of the two T & M Dixon partners, Thomas, in 1857, aged 39, married Jane Heynes of Bromsgrove and they lived at The Cottage, a farmhouse just down Stoney Lane from the Lower House, where now is a private hospital. Jane died, childless, in 1876. Thomas married again, the following year, a cousin, Susannah Walford of the Tack Farm, Tardebigge. She died, also without issue, in 1891. Thomas himself died in 1896, leaving his interest in T & M Dixon to his younger brother Matthew. In memory of his two wives Thomas had a fine stained-glass window, designed and made by the Bromsgrove Guild, put into Tardebigge Church.

Thomas and Mary Dixon (second generation)

16

The Governor, Matthew Dixon

Matthew Dixon, 12 years younger than Thomas, long out-lived him, and died in 1924 at the age of 93. In 1857 he married Anne Walford, daughter of Matthew and Elizabeth Walford of Birmingham. They lived at The Lower House and brought up a family of ten children, five girls and five boys, the boys being educated at Bromsgrove School. When his brother Thomas died in 1896, Matthew became the sole proprietor and was soon affectionately and respectfully known as "The Governor". He was assisted by his eldest son Matthew who moved into The Cottage and who, because of his distinguished career as a commissioned officer in the 2nd Volunteer Battalion of the Worcestershire Regiment, became known as Colonel Dixon.

T & M Dixon Limited Under the Governor, 1900-24

In 1900, perhaps with a view to expansion as well as to forestall the burden of death duty on personal estate, the Governor decided to turn T & M Dixon into a limited liability company. According to a report in the Bromsgrove Messenger of 19 January 1901, the Company, T & M Dixon Ltd., had just been registered "with a capital of £30,000, in 20,000 ordinary shares of £1 each, and 2,000 preference shares of £5 each, to acquire and carry on the business of a coal, coke, lime, and corn merchant and farmer, carried on at Redditch, Tardebigge and elsewhere, and at Paradise Street and elsewhere in Birmingham, by M.Dixon." This business was initially firmly in the hands of the Governor and owned by members of his family, including his sons Matthew, Hugh, Ralph and Arthur, and his daughter Elizabeth Thompson. The first directors were The Governor himself (Chairman), Col. Dixon, and Hugh Dixon. At an early stage the capital was increased to include, beside the 20.000 ordinary shares, 9,000 $5^{1}/_{2}\%$ redeemable debentures (all owned by the Governor) and 17,500 6% cumulative first preference shares of £5.

Under the new Company there was further expansion. The farming operation was greatly extended. Besides the Lower house, The Cottage and Horns Hall Farm, other farms soon rented from the Hewell Estates were Stoney Lane Farm, Hollow Tree Farm, and Tutnall House Farm. Land was also rented on the east side of the Canal from the Old Wharf towards Shortwood Tunnel for an extensive piggery and poultry farm.

A Worcestershire Dynasty

T & M Dixon - the business partners Thomas and Matthew Dixon

In addition, The Governor owned Burcot House Farm, Ashborough's Farm (also known as Burcot Farm) in Burcot Lane, and the Dust House Farm. Altogether some 3,000 acres were being farmed by the 1920s. In addition to the coal and timber business with an office at Hewell Road, Redditch, depots and offices continued to be maintained at Studley, Bromsgrove, Barnt Green Station, Kings Norton, Harborne and at Camp Hill, Birmingham.

From the outset T & M Dixon Limited were involved in mixed farming. On the arable side corn was grown and also vegetables and flowers. On the dairy side there was a herd of pedigree Shorthorn cattle that were tuberculin tested from about 1904. and the milk went by canal boat into Birmingham and was supplied to the General Hospital there. Adjoining the Old Wharf, by this time known as Dixons' Wharf, there was an intensive piggery with about 1,000 pigs; and one of the lime kilns by the canal winding hole had been converted into a slaughterhouse and the other into a sty for sows. Some 25,000 hens occupied special henhouses or roamed the fields between the Wharf and Shortwood tunnel. In the 1920s and 30s sheep were kept around Hollow Tree farm.

Mr. Best, the occupier of Stoney Lane Farm before Dixons rented it, had been interested in soft-fruit growing, and this was developed in a big way by Ralph Dixon when he moved in, with strawberries, raspberries, blackcurrants, redcurrants and gooseberries, being grown to supply markets as far away as London. In the early 1920s, near to Dixons' new offices at Broad Green a fruit-packing depot was established, also an egg-packing shed. Mushrooms were grown indoors and also on ridges outdoors at Broad Green. Soft fruit was sent by rail from Blackwell Station for the London markets and elsewhere. At fruit-picking time many people from the Black Country came out for several weeks and camped in barns at the Dusthouse, Lower House and Stoney Lane Farms.

It seems to have been the original intention of the Governor that only his eldest son, Col. Dixon, should go into the business. His second son Thomas qualified as a doctor and practised as one. The third son Hugh Walford Dixon began a banking career, but soon persuaded his father to let him join the farming business as a Director. The fourth son Ralph qualified as a chartered accountant, practised for a few years in Redditch, and then, being the apple of his father's eye, he also managed to persuade the Governor to take him into the farming business and to become a Director. The fifth and youngest son Harvey became a dentist and practised in Birmingham. So eventually three of the five sons, Col. Matthew, Hugh and Ralph, were actively involved in the business and they continued to run it jointly following the death of their father in 1924.

The death of the Governor, aged 93, in 1924 marked the end of an era, for his oversight and control of the business had continued almost to the end. Like many other members of the Dixon family he was a very tall man and well built, he was a strict disciplinarian and expected all his family and his employees to maintain high standards of honesty and efficiency. He played a prominent part in local affairs and was a regular attender and supporter of his Parish Church. Up to within a year of his death he used to ride round on his horse to inspect his farms and see that they were being efficiently run.

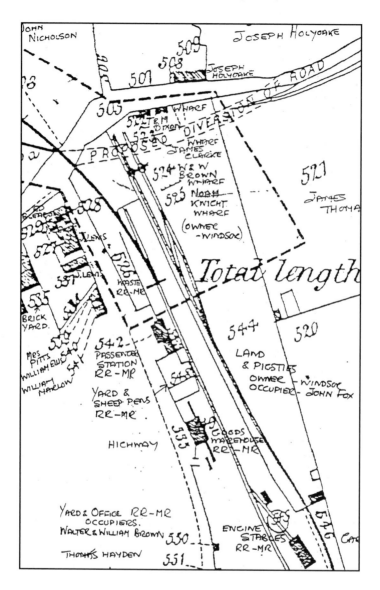

Part of the 1862 plan of the proposed Evesham and Redditch Railway where it would join the terminus of the existing Redditch Railway. The names of owners and tenants of the coal wharf at the Hewell Road end of the goods yard. RR-MR indicates the Redditch Railway leased to the Midland Railway. The Dixon tenancy of location 522 is described as Wharf, Machine House, Office etc., Owner Windsor, Occupier T & M Dixon.

Dixons' Use of Canal and Rail Transport

Until the early 1900s Dixons fleet of some 50 canal boats, mostly day boats, carried coal and other commodities such as hay, manure and limestone, and this business was then run from the Old Wharf, Bridge Street, off Gas Street Basin in Birmingham, as well as from Dixon's Wharf, Tardebigge. The fleet of boats was run down as rail and road transport was increasingly used. By the 1920s and 1930s only four or five boats remained in use. In 1905 a special canal boat, *Enterprise*, was constructed for Dixons at George Farrin's Boatyard, Stoke Prior. It was designed by Francis Hobrough, Engineer of the Worcester and Birmingham Canal Company, and it was the first motor canal boat in the country, being driven by a Wolseley car engine. It could carry 15 tons and was able to make the journey into Birmingham in $3\frac{1}{2}$ hours, as against the 7 hours taken by horse-drawn boats. It left Tardebigge Old Wharf in the early morning with milk, fruit, vegetables, eggs and poultry, and returned in the afternoon with a mixed cargo. The *Enterprise* was crewed at first by George Colledge and his brother-in-law Jack Lewin. then by Ernest Jones of Tutnall and Tom Lewin. It ran for many years into the early 1930s until superseded by motor transport. It lay at the Old Wharf for a time and then, after sinking, spent 2 years under water before Ralph Dixon had it raised and the engine, after being renovated at Dixon's Redditch Garage by mechanic George Cole, was used to work a water pump at the Old Wharf.

The Redditch coal business was supplied by rail to Dixons' own double siding which could accommodate about 25 wagons and which joined the main line beyond the engine shed and ran parallel to and below the railway embankment. Dixons had their own named railway wagons, some of which brought in timber as well as coal. Besides using the railway sidings at their Hewell Road Wharf, Dixons also had coal delivered by rail to Barnt Green and sold and delivered coal from there, and they sent off orchard and soft fruit countrywide from Blackwell sidings in the 1920s, 1930s and 1940s.

From 1924 Under Colonel Matthew, Hugh and Ralph Dixon

Following the death of their father the three brothers managed the business empire on into the 1930s, but under increasing difficulties as the recession of the late 1920s and early 1930s took hold. During the

Matthew and Anne Dixon and their family circa 1897. From left to right, top row: Ralph, Matthew, Grace, Thomas, Hugh, Harry Thompson (husband of Annie); centre: Matthew and Anne Dixon; bottom row: Elizabeth (Thompson), her son Reg, Arthur Harvey, Jane, Annie.

1914-18 War, a subsidiary company, T & M Dixon (Farmers) Ltd., had been formed with a capital of 100 £1 shares of which the Governor and his sons Matthew, Hugh and Ralph held one share each, the remaining 96 shares being owned by the parent Company, T & M Dixon Ltd. The purpose of this was to mitigate the tax liabilities arising from the large profits made by the farming and other businesses during the War. In 1927, three years after the Governor's death, the three brothers, at a Board Meeting, sold themselves the 96 shares owned by the parent Company. By this means they obtained complete control of the farming side of the business, leaving T & M Dixon Ltd. as a separate Company with its coal, timber and garage interests. Besides T & M Dixon (Farmers) Ltd., a further business, T & M Dixon (Farmers), a partnership and not a limited company, was formed in the 1930s.

Of the three brothers, Colonel Dixon, a big man like his father and brothers, remained a bachelor. Although becoming Chairman of the T & M Dixon Companies, he was less actively involved than his brothers, having many other interests, but he was in overall charge of the coal business whilst it continued to be centred at the Old Wharf. He lived at The Cottage and made a home there for his widowed sister Elizabeth Thompson and her family. He had joined the the 2nd. Volunteer Battalion of the Worcestershire Regiment in 1880, and after a long and distinguished career in the Volunteer and Territorial Armies, he retired from service as Lieut.-Col. in 1911. He again served as Colonel in the Worcestershire Regiment in the Great War until forced to retire due to ill health in 1916. He was a Deputy-Lieutenant and a Justice of the Peace for Worcestershire, sitting on the Bromsgrove Bench, and he was awarded the Victorian Decoration for his long and meritorious service in the Volunteer and Territorial forces. He was a keen sportsman, he hunted, and was a first class game shot, and one of his interests was the breeding and training of flat-coated retriever gun dogs. He owned a chauffer-driven Austin 20 with an enormous body which had been specially built for him (he was a big man) but he usually rode around the farms on horseback. He died, after a long illness, in 1932.

Hugh Walford Dixon was married in 1903 to his cousin Mabel Walford and they lived at The Elbows in Hewell Lane. They had no children and Mabel long outlived her husband, becoming a J.P. Hugh's banking experience was no doubt of use in dealing with the financial side of the business. His farming interest was chiefly in livestock and horses, and he was particularly involved with the production and marketing of milk. He was an active member of the Farmers' Union, serving on various of its committees, and was highly regarded in farming circles. He was Vicar's Warden at St. Bartholomew's Church, Tardebigge, for 16 years and served on the Parish Council of Tutnall and Cobley. As Secretary and organiser of the annual Whit-Monday Fete at Hewell he helped to make it one of the most popular Bank-holiday events in the Midlands. He was the first of the three brothers in the business to die, in 1931.

The Governor (Matthew Dixon)

The third brother, Ralph Dixon, was the one whose ideas and initiative brought about many changes in the farming business. He was also behind the expansion of the trade in coal, timber and building materials in Redditch and the development of the garage there. Married in 1902 to Florence Ida Tombs, daughter of the Town Clerk of Droitwich, he built The Hollow Tree House at Vigo to be their home.

A History of the Family Business

Because, like many of the Dixons he was very tall (6ft 7in in his case) the doors were made 7ft high to provide extra headroom. Around 1914 Ralph and his family moved into Stoney Lane Farm which remained the family home until World War 2.

Ralph was a kind, fatherly man, very strong, and with boundless energy. He was seen riding a bicycle carrying an iron horse plough over his shoulder, and he could easily lift a model T Ford car round, one end at a time. He had many ideas for improving the efficiency and profitability of the farming enterprise and must have persuaded his ageing father to agree to various innovations, such as the sale of the dairy herd and the end of milk distribution about 1921, the cessation of corn growing about 1923, and their replacement by an expansion of the poultry, pig, and fruit-growing sides of the farming operation, in which he was specially interested. Of an inventive turn of mind, he designed labour-saving poultry houses and also a corrugated-iron adjustable rick or timber stack cover. The intensive piggery adjacent to the Old Wharf was served by a 2 feet gauge tramway by which waste food and manure, brought from Birmingham markets and Davenport's Brewery by canal boat, were transported to the sties. He was the owner of one of the first £100 Ford cars, and often stopped to give lifts to women at a time when this was an unquestioned act of courtesy. Ralph was responsible for developing what was widely known as the "Worcestershire Poultry Farm" covering a large area; but perhaps his greatest achievement was the development of the fruit-growing side of the farming business into one of the largest in Great Britain, with an extensive acreage of soft fruit, apples and pears, carefully graded and packed at Burcot and Broad Green, and distributed countrywide via road and rail. He showed great concern for the welfare of the Black Country folk who came annually to stay and gather in the fruit harvest, and he was highly regarded by them. On the death of his brother Col. Dixon in 1932 Ralph become Chairman of T & M Dixon Ltd. and of T & M Dixon (Farmers) Ltd. and the senior partner of T & M Dixon (Farmers). He died in 1936, the last of the three brothers in the business.

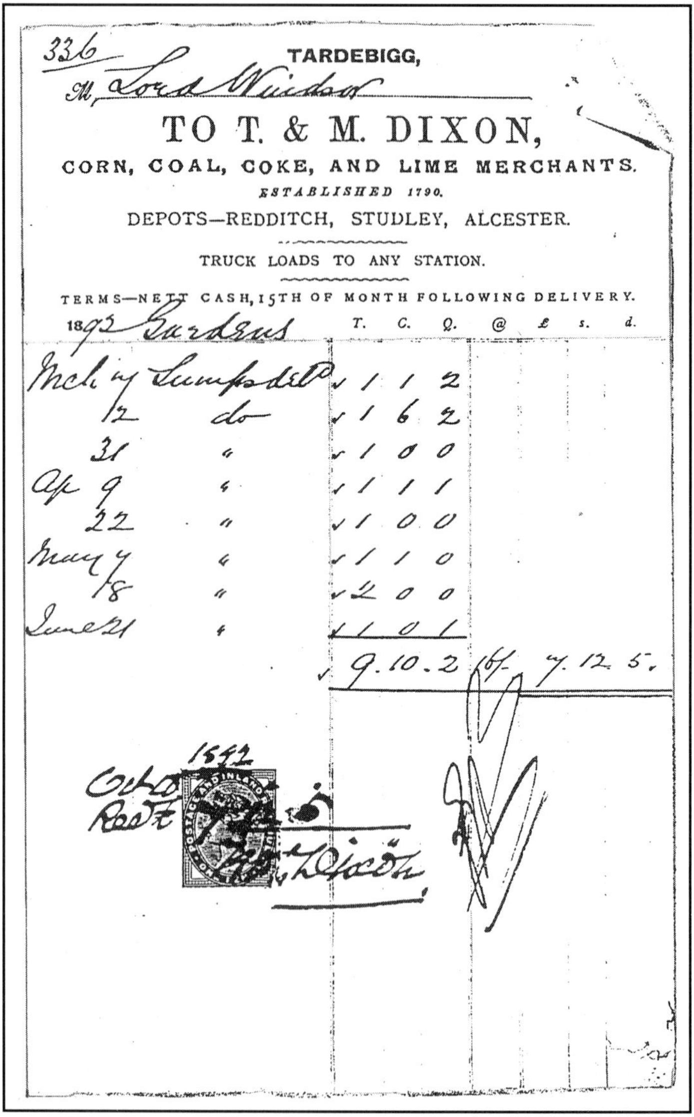

336

TARDEBIGG,

M. Lord Windsor

TO T. & M. DIXON,

CORN, COAL, COKE, AND LIME MERCHANTS.

ESTABLISHED 1790.

DEPOTS—REDDITCH, STUDLEY, ALCESTER.

TRUCK LOADS TO ANY STATION.

TERMS—NETT CASH, 15TH OF MONTH FOLLOWING DELIVERY.

1892 Gardens	T.	C.	Q.	@	£	s.	d.
Mch 7 Lumps delivd	1	1	2				
12 do	1	6	2				
31 "	1	0	0				
Ap 9 "	1	1	1				
22 "	1	0	0				
May 7 "	1	1	0				
18 "	2	0	0				
June 21 "	1	0	1				
	9	10	2	16/-	7	12	5

1542

Recd

Dixon

Bill for coal supplied by Dixons to Lord Windsor, 1892.

Dixons' Offices and Administration

Until just after the First World War the farming business had been
run from offices at the various farm houses, by the Governor from the
Lower House, by Ralph Dixon from Stoney Lane Farm, and by Colonel
Dixon (mainly the Old Wharf coal business) from The Cottage. After
the War, Dixons purchased an ex-army hospital building from the
London area and had it erected at Broad Green in 1920-21 for use as
their main offices. For sixty years the Accountant Clerk for T & M
Dixon (Farmers) and the succeeding company Tardebigge Orchards
was Jack Houghton. He worked in their offices from leaving Tardebigge
School in 1911 at the age of 14 until he retired in 1971.

Dixons had another office at their Hewell Road Wharf in Redditch,
situated behind the two terraced houses to the right of the wharf gate.
Ernald Dixon, son of Dr Thomas Dixon, worked there as Company
Secretary from 1920 to 1931. There was also an office used by Dixons in
the Coal Exchange at the corner of New Street and Corporation Street in
Birmingham.

The Final Years of the T & M Dixon Farming Business

Following Ralph's death the farming business of T & M Dixon
(Farmers) continued under the partnership and management of
Howard Bird, Allan Macdonell and Bill Thompson. Howard Bird had
been originally employed as Company Secretary in T & M Dixon's
Office at Broad Green. His long and efficient service was eventually
rewarded by his being allowed by Ralph Dixon to invest in T & M
Dixon and to become a director of the coal business and a partner in the
farm business. Allan Macdonell (1905-54) came as a young man to learn
about farming from Ralph Dixon. He married Ralph's eldest daughter
Honor in 1928 and they lived at The Cottage following Colonel Dixon's
death in 1932. William Noel Ayscough (Bill) Thompson was a son of the
Governor's eldest daughter Annie who had married her cousin Henry
Ayscough Thompson, and so he was a cousin of Ralph Dixon's sons,
Matthew, Peter and Crispian Dixon. He and his wife and family lived at
Burcot Farm.

Of Ralph's sons, Matthew (born 1911) was not interested in farming
and he moved away from Tardebigge to live eventually in London.
Crispian (born 1914), on leaving school, entered the business and

Colonel Matthew Dixon

worked mainly on the poultry side. In 1937 Peter (born 1918), together with Howard Bird's son John, also joined the farming business as a student. Peter, after distinguished war service in which he gained the Military Cross, was killed in action in March 1945. There is a memorial window to him in Tardebigge Church. A further tragedy occurred when Crispian, who had personal problems, took his own life in 1948.

During the second world war, 1939-45, and immediately following, T & M Dixon (Farmers) were kept extremely busy as food production was a vital priority. All available land was utilised. Soon after the beginning of the war, in 1940, Dixons ploughed up Blackwell Golf Course, apart from the greens, for food production, and it continued to be farmed until 1947 when they reseeded it. Dixons had long enjoyed a right of way along a track over the golf course as a short cut for taking produce to Blackwell Station. Although some agricultural workers were exempt from military service, manpower was augmented by the services of four members of the Women's Land Army, Mary Godrich, Margaret Hall, Christine Galletly and Nellie Myatt (who was later headmaster's secretary at Bromsgrove School in the time of Headmaster Lionel Carey). Italian prisoners of war were also brought in to help, as on other farms in the area.

Following World War 2 changes began to take place which led to the end of the businesses of T & M Dixon under that name. One major event affecting the farms was the sale of the Hewell Estate at Tardebigge by the Plymouth family in 1946 caused by their having to pay heavy death duties and by their decision to move to their remaining family home, Oakley Park near Ludlow. A consortium of four, Joe Beckett, Howard Bird, Dr Houfton and John Coney, purchased all but Hewell Grange and its grounds (acquired by the Home Office for a Borstal Institution). They then sold off many of the farms to the various tenant farmers. Some of the T & M Dixon farms which had been rented from the Plymouth Estates passed into the ownership of Howard Bird at that time and their fields remained part of the still extensive terrain of the T & M Dixon (Farmers) partnership.

After the War, John Bird, who was most actively involved in managing the farms, was keen to extend the orchards and to concentrate on the growing of apples and pears. So around 1948 the soft fruit acreage began to to be greatly reduced, the dairy, pig and poultry

Ralph Dixon

businesses began to be phased out and much of the farm land was converted to orchards. It was at this time that Stoney Lane Farm and Robin Hill Farm (formerly Horns Hall), both owned by T & M Dixon (Farmers), were sold to raise money to build the cold stores and other facilities needed for processing, grading and packing the apples and pears. During the 1950s and 1960s the orchards, with their ordered rows of apple and pear trees, covered a vast area including the fields below Tardebigge Church and by the side of the old Bromsgrove to Redditch Road, and in the Spring the trees in blossom, viewed from Tardebigge churchyard, were a beautiful sight. There were about 50,000 fruit trees covering some 600 acres.

Following World War 2 the partnership of Howard Bird, Allan Macdonell and Bill Thompson in T & M Dixon (Farmers) continued until 1952 when it was decided to terminate the partnership and form a company, Tardebigge Orchards Limited. The directors of this new company were Allan Macdonell, Howard Bird and his son John Bird, Bill Thompson and an accountant Ken Jones. From this time the apples and pears were sold under the brand name TOR. With the creation of Tardebigge Orchards the long farming enterprise of Dixons of Tardebigge formally came to an end, although Bill Thompson, a member of the Dixon family continued to be involved.

In 1954 Allan Macdonell died and his share in the partnership passed to his estate. He and his wife Honor had lived at The Cottage from 1932, when Col. Matthew died. Following Allan's death, Honor decided to move and ownership of The Cottage then passed out of the Dixon family, it being eventually converted into a private hospital for cosmetic surgery. The policy of concentrating on orchard fruit, though successful for some years, proved in the end to be disastrous due to French competition in the 1960s. By that time French farmers, in line with their government's policy and with financial help from their government, were producing apples intensively at 24 tons to the acre, whereas the output of Tardebigge Orchards was only about 7 tons to the acre. The French were dumping apples in this country, selling at a shilling a pound, whereas best English apples such as Cox's cost upwards of 1s 6d per pound. As a result of the slump in orchard fruit sales Tardebigge Orchards, about 1971, decided to sell off the business. The Macdonell family wished to receive their one-third share of the proceeds and it was therefore decided that all the property owned by the company should be sold by auction and that one-third of the proceeds should go to each of Howard Bird, John Bird and the Macdonell family. John Bird then purchased the Lower House Farm and the Dusthouse Farm lands and his son Christopher Bird purchased Ashborough's Farm which had been in the ownership of the Dixon family since the turn of the century and latterly part of Tardebigge Orchards. With the help of Ray King, John Bird continued farming fruit for a few years and then converted the land to arable farming, still under the business name of Tardebigge Orchards, until 1995. The growing of soft fruit continued at Ashborough's Farm

Dixons' horsedrawn boat Snowdrop tied up beside the old warehouse and coal stacked on Tardebigge Old Wharf. The bathers were Tom King and Bernard Bloomer.

Dixons' new motor-boat Enterprise at Farrins' Dock, Stoke Works, in 1906.

until 1995. Howard Bird who withdrew from the farming scene in 1971 died in 1973. Bill Thompson, who severed his connection with Tardebigge Orchards in its early years died in 1984.

The Final Years of T & M Dixon Limited

The coal and coke business of T & M Dixon Ltd. continued until after World War 2, based at Tardebigge and Redditch, and with depots and offices in Station Road, Studley, and at Barnt Green Station. There was also an office in Navigation Street, Birmingham, for coal, cement and builders' materials. During World War 2 Dixons contracted to construct air strips, and following the War they were advertising as suppliers, from Barnt Green, of, besides coal, also cement, sand, crazy paving, rockery and walling stone, and as contractors for drive making and tar spraying.

By 1938, Dixons' annual sale of coal was 136,000 tons, of which about half went directly to the Austin Motor Company at Longbridge to heat their factory. Most of the coal came from Coventry and Nottingham pits; some (steam coal) from S.Wales. Eventually the coal business was sold about 1964 to British Anthracite. The last manager of the Coal business was Norman Cook. He had worked for Dixons since leaving school, first at Tardebigge, then, at the Hewell Road, Redditch, Wharf where he succeeded Benjamin Huntley as coal manager.

The timber business of T & M Dixon Ltd. at Hewell Road, Redditch, continued for many years until it came to an end in the early 1950s. Much of the uncut timber came by rail, some from overseas, and it was unloaded and transported across the coal and timberyard to the sawmill by a large gantry crane. Tree trunks also came by road from woodlands in the Tardebigge area. Sawn timber was stacked high for seasoning. There was a wheelwright's shop and a shoeing forge in the early years, and a carpenters' shop which produced such things as portable buildings, poultry houses, fencing, barrows, ladders, gates and the decks of lorries. Six wooden bungalows had been erected at the far end of the Wharf; these were rented by Dixons' employees and were there until after World War 2.

On 26 November 1925 there was a disastrous fire in the timberyard which began in the early hours. It destroyed the sawmill and machinery and hundreds of tons of sawn timber. Damage was also done to the overhead crane, the girders supporting which were twisted almost beyond recognition by the heat. A steam fire engine was soon on the scene and fortunately the spectacular blaze, which lit up the countryside for miles around, was confined to one end of the timberyard. The damage was soon rectified and the business resumed.

Until the early 1900s Dixons relied, for road transport, on their fleet of horse-drawn vehicles, carts and wagons, and there were coach houses and stables on the farms and also at the Hewell Road Depot. But by the 1920s Dixons had five steam lorries of which three were Sentinels and two Yorkshire transverse-boiler types. These were soon supplemented by Austin petrol-engined lorries which, during the 1930s, took their place. To service the steam and petrol lorries a repair garage was set up at Hewell Road between the main gate and the railway. It was around 1925 that T & M Dixon Ltd., then chaired by Ralph Dixon, became Agents for Austin Cars and the garage was rebuilt and extended. They also branched out into the transport business, carrying other people's goods besides their own. Following Ralph Dixon, managing directors of the Garage were, as already mentioned, Howard Bird and Bill Thompson. For many years, from the late 1920s until 1971 the garage manager was Frank Allwood; he lived in a house between the garage and the railway bridge. Chief Mechanic from 1929 onwards was Arthur Cole. He serviced vehicles, not only at Redditch, but also at the various houses and farms of the Dixons. Just after the end of World War 2, T & M Dixon Ltd. took over the garage and petrol-filling station of Portman and Allbutt in Easemore Road, Redditch, and this was run jointly with the Hewell Road business under Frank Allwood.

The Garages comprised the last remaining business of T & M Dixon Ltd., and the Company was finally sold in April 1972 to Studley Garage and Engineering Works Ltd., who paid face value for the preference shares, repaid the debentures in full, and paid £3.50 each for the ordinary shares. They also undertook to retain all Dixons' employees. Following the sale of the business Arthur Cole continued for six years as chief mechanic for the new owner, Roger Hill, proprietor of the Studley Firm, and retired when the garage, still trading as T & M Dixon, finally closed in 1978.

The last member of the Dixon family to work for the family business was Harry Thompson, son of Bill Thompson. Harry served as an apprentice at the Hewell Road garage in the 1950s. then, after national service in the RAF and experience elsewhere, returned to work in the service department of the garage, continuing under Roger Hill until the garage closed.

So ended what had been, in its heyday, a thriving business empire, employing many local people, and supplying people near and far with coal and coke, lime, timber and other building materials, also farm produce, grain and animal feeds, meat, eggs, milk, fruit, vegetables and flowers, and finally cars.

Chapter Two
Tardebigge in the 1920s

The late W. Dudley Thompson (1916-1993), one of the four children of Reg and Ruth Thompson, lived with his parents at the Hollow Tree House, Vigo, from the age of two until the age of sixteen. The following slightly edited account is the last section of a family history which he wrote, and his memories provide a fascinating insight into life in the Tardebigge area and into T & M Dixon's farming business and the people involved in it in the 1920s.

The period in which I lived in the parish, from 1918 to 1932, was remarkable because it included the last few years of the spacious days of farming, the depression of the late 20s and early 30s and the start of the mechanisation which was eventually to replace the heavy horse as the motive power in British agriculture.

In the early years of this century that part of Tardebigge lying to the west of the Worcester and Birmingham Canal was virtually a Dixon family village, although most of the farms were actually rented from the Earl of Plymouth's Hewell Estate. At the Lower House, the hub of both family and farms, lived my great grandfather Matthew Dixon (The Governor) with his daughter and son-in-law, Jane and Basil Housman, and his only unmarried daughter Grace Dixon. Active partners in the business with him were his eldest son, Colonel Matt Dixon, who lived at The Cottage with his widowed sister (my grandmother) Bess Thompson, and two other sons, Hugh Dixon, who with his wife Mabel lived at The Elbows (once the village pub), and Ralph Dixon, who with his wife Ida and their five children, lived at Stoney Lane Farm. In addition there were three of the Governor's grandsons working in the firm and living at Tardebigge and these were:- my father Reg Thompson living at Hollow Tree House with his wife Ruth and four children; Noel (Bill) Thompson (the youngest son of great grandfather's eldest daughter Annie) living with his wife Mary at Burcot House (they were married in 1926 and their three children were born in the late 20s and early 30s); and Ernald Dixon, the younger son of Dr Tom Dixon, who with his wife Marjorie lived in a house near the Oxleasowes Farm.

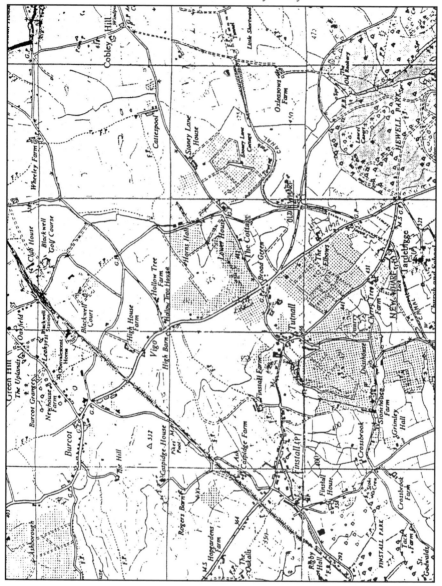

T & M Dixon farming country, showing the extent of the orchards around 1950.
Scale 2½ inches to the mile.

Bill Thompson joined the business before the First World War; he was mainly involved with the fruit orchards. After the war my father Reg Thompson took over the management of the Worcestershire Poultry Farm, and Ernald Dixon joined the firm in the Redditch office and became secretary of T & M Dixon Ltd.

Three other farm houses were occupied by key farm staff. At Hollow Tree Farm, just along the lane from our house, lived the shepherd John Evans (one of his daughters, Alice, was a maid at The Lower House) and the farm buildings there were used mainly in connection with the flock of grass sheep. At Horns Hall lived the farm foreman, George Knight; and at The Dust House was the gamekeeper whose name was Marshall. In two houses at the poultry farm lived Joseph Pitson who was the Colonel's chauffeur (his daughter Margaret was one of the maids at The Cottage) and John Johnson, then retired, who had been the manager of the poultry farm before my father took over in 1918. At Broad Green were the farm offices, the forge which was run by Ted Tustin and his son Harry, the laundry and another cottage in which lived one of the horsemen, George Powell, who had two crippled children, Jackie and Dolly, who were both permanently in wheel chairs. At the Old Wharf were several farm cottages, one of which was occupied by a dear old lady named Elizabeth Green who did sewing work at the various family houses, the village shop which was kept by Mr and Mrs Davis (he was an ex-naval man and was the gardener at The Cottage) and the big intensive piggery together with a very primitive slaughter house. Scattered about the various farms were several other farm cottages, usually in pairs, and these were all occupied by farm staff whose children, when old enough, found work either on the farms, in the office, or in one or other of the family houses.

I was born in February 1916 and my earliest memory of Tardebigge dates from before we went to live there in 1918 and must have been an occasion when we were staying with my grandmother at The Cottage. The garden there included a tennis lawn large enough for three courts side by side, and this was ploughed up to grow vegetables during the Great War. I have a vivid recollection of sitting in my pram in the summer house and watching the head horseman, George Skillern, ploughing the tennis courts with a pair of horses and a single-furrow plough. I cannot at that time have known the identity of the ploughman

The forecourt of the Birmingham Canal Navigation offices at the Old Wharf, Birmingham. The coal cart nearest the camera bears the name T & M Dixon. Dixons had an extensive coal business in Birmingham.

but when I was older and came to know all the farm men by name I was always aware that it was George Skillern whom I had watched that day.

My earliest memory of The Hollow Tree must have been in the summer of 1918 or 1919. It is of watching German prisoners of war who worked on the farms marching past our house in the evenings on the way back to their billets at The Dust House. There was also an occasion when my elder sister, Elisabeth, and I were taken for a picnic in one of the hay fields near The Hollow Tree where the Germans were loading hay wagons. One of them was moved to tears at the sight of us enjoying ourselves in the hay, and the maid who was with us - I think it was Ethel Tranter from Vigo - told us that she thought that he was thinking of his own children far away in Germany and wondering when he would be able to see them again.

Tardebigge in the 1920s

When we were young there was endless pleasure in being taken for walks as there was hardly any motor traffic to worry us and many of the lanes were not even tarred, so that the banks and hedges were full of wild flowers, birds and small animals. All we met in our travels were a few farm carts and relatives or acquaintances on horseback. Great Grandpa, uncle Matt, uncle Hugh and our cousin Honor Dixon all rode regularly and there were several other local riders that we knew by name as, of course, we did the various farm men whom we met in our travels. There was, however, a Sentinel steam wagon belonging to the local millers and a steam roller used when the main roads were being retarred, both of which I found rather frightening when I was small.

But there was another sort of steam engine of which I had no fear at all but only a great fascination. Only a few minutes walk from our house the road down to Burcot passed under the main LMS railway line from Birmingham to Worcester, and at this spot there was a footpath up to the line and a stile from which one could watch the trains going by. There could not have been a better rural spot for train watching for this was a busy line and the stile was about half way down the Lickey Incline which was the steepest railway gradient on the English main-line railway system. From the stile one could look up the line to Blackwell Station (our local halt) where every down train, including the through expresses, had to stop to check the brakes before going down the bank. Most of the goods trains of that time were hand braked, and the brake gang at Blackwell would pin down a number of the brakes before the train pulled over the top of the bank (if they had put on too many brakes while the train was still on the flat it would have been unable to start) and then as it gathered speed the brake men ran beside the train pinning down extra brakes until the train was under control. Sometimes the locked wheels would come past the stile with a shower of sparks coming from the rails and probably a flat on the tyre by the time the train reached Bromsgrove Station.

For the up trains Bromsgrove engine shed held several 0-6-0 tank engines and one beautiful 0-10-0 tender engine, numbered 2290 and known as Big Bertha, which I believe was the only one of its kind. These were bank engines which helped to push trains up the gradient. 2290 was powerful enough on her own but the smaller engines were often used in pairs. It was a wonderful sight to watch a heavy train

Aerial view of Tardebigge Church and the New Wharf. Dixons used the old large stone warehouse beside the canal as a grist mill for the production of animal and poultry feeds.

coming up the bank with all the engines on full regulator and clouds of steam and red hot ash coming from the chimneys and, by contrast, a down express with hardly a sound except perhaps the whisper of escaping steam at the safety valve, racing down the bank at full speed.

Our family had no motor car; both father and mother rode pushbikes, so most of our shorter journeys were done on foot or else we walked to Tutnall to catch the Midland Red bus to Bromsgrove or Redditch. Sometimes we had rides in the ancient Lower House car driven by George Smith. If we were going into Birmingham we either went by train from Blackwell Station or in The Cottage car driven by Joseph Pitson which took Uncle Matt into the Birmingham office every Thursday. The train journeys were remarkable for the pomp and ceremony with which mother was greeted on arrival at Blackwell by Mr Mellor, the station master, resplendent in his frock coat and best uniform cap, and the masterly way in which mother would always turn this to our advantage. Unless there was a completely empty 3rd class compartment directly in front of us when the train stopped, which was not often the case in those days, she would say 'The train's very full today, Mr Mellor', upon which he would at once usher us into an empty 1st class compartment and lock the door so that we should not be disturbed before reaching Birmingham. I cannot recall her ever playing the same trump at New Street for the return journey, though I am quite sure she would have done so - and pulled it off - had she felt it necessary. Another abiding memory of those journeys was the rush to pull up the windows when going through the five tunnels leading into New Street Station, and the clouds of acrid smoke and grit which filled the compartment if one was a moment too late in closing them.

On some special occasions, mostly I think when going to parties at other houses or in the Village Hall, when we were all dressed up, we went in a hired Victoria which was driven by an old man who lived down Vigo. If it was fine I usually managed to ride on the box seat

Aerial view of The Elbows. This house and farm in Hewell Lane, surrounded by fields of fruit bushes and trees, was the home of Hugh Dixon and his wife Mabel. It had been an ale house in the nineteenth century.

which was a great excitement but, because in childhood I suffered with asthma and hay fever (mainly brought on by proximity to horse or hay and thus not the most convenient ailment when living on a farm), this usually resulted in my arrival at the party with streaming eyes and nose.

Tardebigge Old Wharf. Dixons' coal wharf was on the right of the canal in this view from the road bridge.

Every Sunday morning we walked to Matins at St. Bartholomew's, Tardebigge, which seemed an awful long way when I was small, and on the return journey all the various families stopped at The Elbows where Uncle Hugh and Aunt Mabel provided very welcome refreshment for the children and, I imagine, rather stronger sustenance for the grown-ups. This visit was the high spot of our Sundays and made some compensation for the boredom of the service which was way above my head at that age. Our pew was second from the front on the right of the aisle and had a wrought-iron lamp standard beside it, and this I attempted to climb during the sermon which resulted in my banishment to the gallery at the back of the church. However I was able to overcome this disadvantage by trying to balance my prayer book on the front ledge of the balcony until it eventually dropped onto the heads of the unfortunate worshippers below me. Unfortunately this did not achieve the total exile which I had anticipated but merely led to my return to the front pew under very much stricter supervision.

There were a number of other families with children of about our age, some of whom came every day to The Hollow Tree in term time to lessons with us, so that there were frequent parties or exchange visits to entertain us. Those I can remember still were Peter and Tinker (Crispian) Dixon, our cousins, from Stoney Lane; Jack and Josephine (Jon) Green from The Holyoaks; Simon and Jeremy (Lionel) Green from the Cherry Trees; John and Lucy Horton from Finstall; Ann and Bobby Goodman from Grimley; Ailsa Ludlow from near Barnsley Hall; John, George and Michael Zair from Burcot; and Mary, Joan and Pym Astbury (who were rather older) who lived with uncle Harvey (who was a dentist in Birmingham) and aunt Gladys Dixon at Tutnall House. Our first governess, Phyllis Paine who lived in Station Road, Bromsgrove, was extremely nice and a very good teacher. She later married one of the masters at Bromsgrove School whose surname was Mason. He was a hero of mine because he played Rugby for Bromsgrove and she used to take me to watch some of the home matches that he played in. About the time that I went away to boarding school in 1926 Phyllis left us and was replaced by Miss Wilkinson whom I do not remember very well since I don't think that I had more than about one term with her, but she continued to teach my younger sisters and some other friends until they in turn all went away to school.

All the farms which were rented from Lord Plymouth, together with Burcot, The Dust House and Grimley which were owned by great grandfather, were farmed as a single holding, and this was originally a mixed stock and grain farm but with an increasing acreage of fruit orchards and poultry. After the Great War, in an effort to overcome the depression of the twenties, more and more land was used for fruit and poultry, and grain growing was discontinued completely, while cattle

An aerial photograph showing the canal between the Old Wharf (left) and Shortwood Tunnel (right). The lower House Farm is in the top left-hand corner and the nearby orchards with their ordered rows of fruit trees are clearly seen.

and sheep shared the pastures with the laying flocks, I can remember the last field of corn to be harvested in my time at Tardebigge, probably about 1922 or 1923, for this was in the field directly behind our house. A path was first cut for the binder by some of the men with scythes and then the binder, drawn by a unicorn (a pair of horses on the pole with a single trace horse in front), cut the crop, with a man stationed at each corner with his scythe to stop the corner becoming too sharp for the binder to negotiate, while still more men stooked the sheaves. When only the last acre or so remained, one or two uncles arrived with shot guns to deal with the rabbits which bolted from the last of the standing corn. After drying out on the stook the corn was carried, using several wagons and a gang of men to pitch up the loads, to The Lower House to be ricked under cover in the big dutch barns until threshing time.

The farm buildings at The Lower House comprised the main

carthorse stables for the whole farm with a dozen or more shire horses and one or two vanners for light haulage. There were several horsemen employed, but I can only remember the head horseman, George Skillern, and Sumner and Powell. The latter had in his team a very big bay mare named Flower who was inclined to bite if you did not keep a very close eye upon her. All the time that I lived at Tardebigge the bulk of the farm work was done by horse power; but there was one tractor driven by a girl named Esther Millward (who came as a Land Girl during the war and stayed on until she married in about 1926), and there were two early-model Ford lorries which were used for the longer haulage work and these were driven by George Skillern's two sons, Matt and Bill. Also at The Lower House was a big dutch barn of three bays with the spaces between them roofed over so that loaded wagons could stand there in the dry and to provide room under cover for the threshing drum. These barns held the corn, straw and hay stocks for most of the farms.

At Stoney Lane Farm the main buildings housed the dairy herd to provide milk and cream for all the families and farm staff; and there was a bull yard with two or three loose boxes which housed a stock bull or sometimes two. These were kept tied up all the time in those days and so were usually of uncertain temper. The cowman was George Burton who lived in one of the pair of Stoney Lane Cottages out in the fields between Stoney Lane and the canal. He had a daughter named Olive who was a maid at Stoney Lane. The stone barn at one side of the cow yard was used for cattle feed and there was also a large dutch barn in the rickyard which had been completely covered in and divided internally into cubicles to house some of the fruit-picking gang which came every year from the Black Country, Birmingham, Wolverhampton, etc. in time to start with the strawberry crop in June and often stayed right through to the tree-fruit harvest in September. Another batch of them was housed in the barns at The Dust House. These fruit pickers were part of the great army of unemployed and often came as complete families, the same families coming back year after year and, although the conditions in which they lived in the barns were deplorable by today's standards, they were often much better than those under which they had to live in the city slums. At least they had fresh air and the country, and for most of them it was the nearest approach to a holiday that they could hope for. During the fruit picking the baskets were weighed in the field and payment was made by metal tallies stamped T & M D on one side and the value (1d, 2d etc.) on the other, and these could be exchanged for cash at the farm office.

The main buildings of the poultry farm were in the lane (Agmore Lane) running from The Lower House towards Blackwell, and these comprised a large incubator house (heated by paraffin burners), brooder house, various sheds for feed storage and for egg grading and packing, banks of fattening cages for cockerels together with a feed-cramming machine which was never used after my father took over, and a shed for plucking and dressing table poultry. In addition there was stabling for three or four ponies or cobs which were used in milk floats as transport for the poultry men who looked after the large laying flock spread out over many of the pastures. There was also an ex-army mule which was driven in a light four-wheeled cart and this animal, like most mules, was a most accomplished kicker. If hit with the reins or whip he could manage to get one leg up over the splash board and hack you smartly on the knee; but if you hit him while going uphill he would delay his retaliation until he reached the top and felt the weight of the cart come off the traces - but he never forgot that he owed you one when the time came. On the other side of the lane a couple of small fields had been wired off with 6ft netting to make a number of runs for the pure-bred foundation stock and these pens were all trap nested and recorded so that a lot of work was involved in getting hens out of the nests and making up the records.

Even as late as the 1920s much of the bulk supplies for T & M Dixon arrived at Tardebigge in narrow boats along the canal or 'The Cut' as it was always called. Coal for the Tardebigge households and also for Hewell Grange was unloaded at the Old Wharf and then distributed by horse and cart, while timber for the saw mill at Redditch, if this was imported, sometimes came by water from Bristol or Gloucester. Another frequent cargo at the Old Wharf was manure from the Birmingham railway stables, and this was used first as bedding in the big piggery beside the wharf and later carted out onto the land. At the New Wharf, situated at the south entrance to Tardebigge Tunnel and just below the church, was the farm-feed mill which, again, received raw materials by water from the Severn ports.

Tardebigge in the 1920s

The canal was a continual source of interest when we were young, for it ran between our fields from the Tardebigge Tunnel to Shortwood Tunnel. Most of the narrow boats were pulled by horses, mules or a pair of donkeys, though there were a few which had their own engines and these usually towed a second 'butty' boat. Because of the two tunnels which had no tow paths, steam or motor tugs were kept at the New Wharf, and these ran a regular service every two hours to take a string of boats to the other side of Shortwood tunnel and to bring back Worcester-bound boats. The animals went over the tunnels and along the towpath between them to join the boats at the other end of the tow and were often taken by the children of the boat families.

The tug crew, Percy Hawkins and John Colledge (one of whose daughters, Evelyn, was parlourmaid at the Lower House), were very good to my Dixon cousins and me and allowed us to travel with them whenever we wanted to. They taught us to steer and to stoke the steam boiler and how to start the heavy oil engine of the motor tug with blowlamp and crowbar, and we learnt to know the shallow places in the cut on which one had to be careful not to run aground. The journeys through the dark tunnels, with only a very faint lamp in the bow of the tug and the tiny speck of light which gradually grew into the mouth of the tunnel, were always a little eerie; but the slow and very peaceful passage through the open fields was sheer joy. Birds and animals were seldom frightened by the passing of the boats, and so we saw more of them than if we had been walking on the towpath. The suck of the tug's screw caused the water level in the cut to drop by a foot or so about level with the bows, and this would reveal water rats in their burrows before the following wash covered them over again.

The skill of the boat people in handling their unwieldy craft in the narrow waters of the cut was most impressive, for a loaded narrow boat carries a lot of way and has no astern gear to slow down when entering locks or coming alongside a wharf; yet they always seemed to be able to judge their speed exactly. The usual routine was for the woman to steer the boat while the man walked the towpath with the horse and, since there was only a single towpath, when two boats passed in opposite directions the loaded boat (which was lower in the water) would keep to the towpath side so that the towlines were not entangled. When towing from the path the long towline was attached to a post almost amidships so that the boat was not continually drawn in towards the bank; but boats in the tow of a tug were on a short towline from the bow, while any following boats would all be joined by short lines from the stern of one to the bow of the other. Both the boat families and their craft were always clean and neat, the men and women mostly in a sort of traditional uniform, and the boats and all their equipment were painted in bright colours and decorated with fancy ropework. I never saw horses, mules or donkeys in anything but perfect condition, with harness brasses shining and the traces (made of large wooden beads threaded on stout rope) painted to match the boat, and each with its squat tin feed bucket either slung from the hames or on a bridle so that the horse could feed as he went along.

From the time when I went away to boarding school when I was ten, I spent every minute of my holidays with my two cousins, Peter and Tinker Dixon, and Bert Byron who lived with them at Stoney Lane where his mother was cook. We found so much to amuse and interest us about the farms and the village that we had no need to explore far into the surrounding countryside. We all had .410 shot guns and in winter these provided our main interest, though we could only shoot vermin on most of the farms because the sporting rights belonged to the landlord, the Earl of Plymouth. Unlike most farms in those days there were very few rabbits on our land because the damage they would have done to the fruit orchards necessitated the employment of a full-time gamekeeper, named Marshall, whose job it was to wage continual war on them. We often helped with the rabbit war, but our real enjoyment was in the organised rat hunts. In many of the larger pastures there were a number of big poultry houses which each held some 300 laying hens and these, of course, attracted colonies of rats which took up their abode under the floors. There were no concrete bases and the floors were made from old railway sleepers laid on the bare earth. Whenever a field was being rested and the sheds were empty, a ratting gang would assemble under the command of Uncle Ralph, consisting of several farm men, we four boys, a number of dogs and an old model T Ford truck. The drill was to stop up all the visible outside rat holes except one, and into this was put the end of a hose pipe attached to the exhaust of the Ford which was then started up. A couple of men with guns, or sometimes a couple of us lads, would keep guard for anything which managed to bolt toward the hedge, while the rest of the party armed with sticks, together with the dogs, would brave the fumes in the shed to take up the floor boards and stack them in piles. Many half-gassed rats would bolt during this work and it was never safe to try to lift a floor board with bare hands unless you wanted to get bitten. The last few boards would be absolutely solid with rats and when all had been dispatched with sticks or by the dogs the inside holes would be trodden in and a final good dose of exhaust gas pumped in before the floors were replaced. We never had a blank day, and the biggest bag that I remember was over 700 rats in one day.

The forge at Broad Green was another attraction, though I think that my visits there were usually made alone since a gang of four of us would have got too much in the way and would not have been encouraged. Ted Tustin and his son, Harry, shod all our farm horses and did all the machinery repairs. They also served the Hewell Estate farms and a number of other local farmers. One was always welcome as an extra hand to blow the bellows and to admire the skill with which the two smiths heated and shaped the iron for shoes or spare parts. There seemed to be nothing they could not fashion using the fire, anvil and hammer, all done by eye and by skill.

In summer, during the fruit season, most of our days were spent out on the farms with Uncle Ralph. He had an old model T Ford car from which the back seats had been removed and replaced with a square box truck in which we rode, usually surrounded by baskets of fruit of one sort or another. The soft fruit, strawberries, raspberries, gooseberries and currants, were picked into 2,3 or 4 pound chip baskets and these were sent off by train overnight, mostly to commission agents in the big industrial cities of the north. In the mornings, after a visit to the farm office, Uncle Ralph would go round the various fields where picking was in progress to assess the quality of the crop and to give the field foreman orders about the quantities and the time at which the pick was required to be at Blackwell Station. The afternoons were spent mostly at the station where there would be a number of box cars already arrived ready for us in the up sidings. There we would help with the loading and labelling of the various consignments of fruit as load after load arrived from the fields to be put into the appropriate railway trucks. In the intervals between loads we had the run of the signal box where we were allowed to pull the levers under strict supervision and, eventually, to receive and answer the bell signals from Bromsgrove and Barnt Green, the boxes on either side. Sometimes, if wagons had to be shunted, one of the bank engines from an up train would be held at Blackwell to do this before returning to Bromsgrove and then we would get a ride on the footplate. On one never-to-be-forgotten occasion I managed to get a ride on the big 0-10-0 no. 2290 down to Bromsgrove, returning on one of the next bankers to come up to Blackwell.

I remember my great grandfather, old Matthew Dixon, The Governor. Even when he was more than ninety years old, and indeed up to a short while before his death, he continued to take an active interest in the farms and he was a familiar figure astride his grey cob riding out every day to see what was being done in the fields and lanes. In those days, unlike most farms today, all the hedges, fences and gates were maintained in perfect order. Every field gate was tarred each year to preserve it; but to prevent the tar soiling the old Governor's gloves, the top rail was never tarred but was painted white. These black and white field gates were a distinctive feature of all the Dixon farms and certainly looked very smart.

As a child at Tardebigge in the 1920s I always had the feeling of being part of a big family. There were so many much-loved aunts and uncles, Granny Thompson and various cousins all living within a mile of us. In addition I knew all the staff of the farms, the office and of the family houses, and most of their own families. Although these were the years of the depression and wages were miserably low, I do not believe that in Tardebigge at that time conditions were as bad for our staff as they undoubtedly were in some other farming areas. I do know that all of our families were deeply concerned for the welfare of our staff and their families and that any cases of illness or other hardship were recognised and alleviated as far as possible. It is also a fact that as trading conditions became more difficult and the type of farming had to be altered to cut out the heaviest losses, all of my uncles put back into the business a great deal of their own money rather than cut down on staff and so harm the families who had served them so faithfully for, in many cases, more than a generation. One of the most important things in my upbringing was to learn that everyone in the community is an individual and each is entitled to proper respect and consideration. I always felt that all of the staff were my friends and I know that I learned a great deal from them. Whilst all of us youngsters were always treated with friendliness and respect by the farm and house staff, they were never afraid to correct us when the need arose.

Looking back on that period of sixty years ago I still feel that those were the happiest days of my life.

The Governor (Matthew Dixon) on his white cob.

Chapter Three
The Memoirs of Jack Houghton

Jack Houghton was born in 1897. He went to Tardebigge School and on leaving at the age of 14 he was invited by Ralph Dixon to work as a clerk in the office of T & M Dixon which was then at Stoney Lane Farm. Jack worked there until new offices were erected at Broad Green after the 1914-18 War in the latter part of which he served. Apart from his war service he worked with Howard Bird in the offices at Stoney Lane and Broad Green for some sixty years from 1911 to 1971, for T & M Dixon until 1952 and then for the succeeding business of Tardebigge Orchards.

Jack Houghton standing in front of the Broad Green offices of T & M Dixon. To the left of the entrance were the boardroom and typists' office; to the right were the telephone room and dining room and (off the photograph) the living quarters of the caretaker. Fruit pickers queued at the dining room windows to exchange their tokens for cash.

A Worcestershire Dynasty

In January 1988 Jack wrote his memoirs under the title: "I Remember; my first 90 years 1/10/1897 to 1/10/1987", in which he recalled, first, his working life at Tardebigge, then his experiences as a soldier in the Great War, and finally his family and his upbringing.

Jack's maternal grandfather, John Prentice, lived in Victorian times in a semidetached farm cottage at Broad Green and worked as a shepherd for T & M Dixon. His wife Emma never went to school and, like many people in those days, she could neither read nor write. They had seven children including Jack's mother Annie and her sister Polly, who, when Jack was young, lived with her husband Frank Collins and their two sons in Hewell Lane. Because the cottage, one room up and one down, on the Old Wharf where Jack lived with his mother and grandmother was so cramped he used to spend the evenings at Aunt Polly's and he slept there for several years. Uncle Frank used to maintain the heating system at Hewell Grange; he died in the Great War, as did one of his sons, Jack's cousin Will. One of Jack's mother's brothers, Alf Prentice, worked for Dixons at one of their depots in Birmingham, selling coal.

Jack's father, Fred Houghton, came of a Birmingham family and he and his wife Annie lived in Birmingham where Jack was born. Sadly he died when Jack was only three years old. Annie then had to find work to keep herself and her son and she returned from Birmingham to live with her widowed mother on the Old Wharf and to work at Hewell Grange as a pantry maid. She had to be at the Grange at 6.00 in the morning, walking the lanes in the dark in the winter. Eventually, when Dixons moved to their new offices at Broad Green she was appointed caretaker there and went to live in the accommodation provided in the office building. Jack lived there with his mother until his marriage. One of Jack's uncles, uncle Jim Houghton, was married to a German girl and they had as many as 25 children, so Jack had a great many cousins.

Of his school days at Tardebigge, Jack remembered:

I was educated at Lord Windsor's Elementary School next to the church. The Headmaster was Mr A C Dilkes. He was a good teacher and a great influence on my life. He was good at telling stories and we used to try and persuade him to read stories to us. Canon Dickens was vicar there for 62 years. He used to come and open the school proceedings and he would arrive again at a quarter to four to close the day. He came on certain mornings to spend an hour with us and I remember him talking to me about the Lord's Prayer. Although it was over eighty years ago I remember it clearly; and with the passing of the years I realise the value, the importance of the Lord's Prayer, which is very comprehensive and contains the Christian religion. I also remember being in the choir at Tardebigge and having a seat next to the Vicar. The boy next to me, Jack Wilson, had a superb treble voice. He could fill that church. I often feel that he should have been recorded because he was very outstanding.

In 1916 at the age of nineteen Jack was called up for army service. He was severely wounded by shellfire in the fighting at Passchendaele and a bullet was removed from close to his spine. He recovered back in England and it was in hospital at Ashington in Northumberland that he met and fell in love with Annie. Ten years elapsed before they could afford to get married. Jack was then earning about 50 shillings a week and Annie about £3 a week as a teacher. Their home was at Linthurst, Blackwell, where they had a small orchard and kept poultry.

The following extracts from Jack's memoirs provide a graphic insight into those members of the Dixon family and others who were involved in the family business and a description of the various farming activities they managed:

The Dixons were tenant farmers of the Hewell Estate and belonged to the age of very strict discipline. If anyone made a mistake or neglected something they were told about it and not allowed to get away with it. The father, Mr Dixon senior, lived at Lower House Farm, Tardebigge. He used to ride about the farm on his pony at the age of 93. All the Dixons were good Christian men, but severe discipline was quite the rule of the day. I remember Mr Dixon senior riding round and stopping at a field gate and calling to one of the men "Now listen, there's a thistle the other side of the field". It was all of 500 yards away and he told this man to go and fetch the thistle, to pull it up, including the roots, and bring it back and put it on the gate so that he could see it when he returned. That was his idea of discipline; no question of neglect or letting things go.

Mr Dixon's family consisted of five sons and five daughters. Of the

Howard Robert Bird (1888 - 1973) joined T & M Dixon as a young man and rose to be Chairman and Managing director and subsequently a partner in Tardebigge Orchards. He was active in various spheres of public life, having been for 25 years a Sunday School Teacher and Superintendent of the Methodist Church at Ham Green near Rredditch, a councillor for Redditch Urban District and for Worcestershire County Council, and a member of numerous organisations. He became Lord of the Manor of Bromsgrove in 1946 when the Hewell Estate was sold and he lived latterly at The Elbows, Tardebigge.

sons, Matthew was a colonel in the local volunteers; he was always known as Colonel Dixon and he lived with one of his sisters, Mrs Thompson, at The Cottage, Stoney Lane. Two other brothers, Mr Ralph and Mr Hugh Dixon, managed the farms and the father used to have two flags in the hall so that when he wanted to speak to one of the sons he would have one of the flags put out near the gateway, and when that son came by he had to collect the flag, take it back into the house and go and see his father. They were not expected to pass the flag without going to see the father.

When I went to work in the office at Stoney Lane Farm, Mr Howard Bird was the clerk there. He was eight years older then me. He was an extraordinary fine character and it was a great good fortune for me to be associated with him at the office from a very young age and to have experienced his kindness and character over a very long period. He was a Sunday School teacher in the village where he lived with his father and mother at Old Yar Mill, Feckenham, near Redditch, and he used to cycle to and from there to Tardebigge daily. He was always very careful to be well-dressed and when he arrived at the office he used to take off his cuffs. He had starched cuffs. I have never seen them used by anyone else, but he always wore them and when he arrived at the office he would take them off and put them into a little cupboard near his desk. His character and ability were recognised by the Dixon brothers, who all died in the 1930s. Before Mr Ralph Dixon died in 1936 he appointed Mr Bird to be a Director of the coal business, T & M Dixon Limited, and a partner in the farm business. After his marriage to a Miss Banner, Mr Bird lived in Redditch. He would come over to Tardebigge for the morning and then go back by bus midday to Redditch to deal with the business of T & M Dixon Limited. He became interested in council work, becoming a member of Redditch Council and eventually a member of Worcestershire County Council.

Mr Howard Bird was a good-looking man. In his younger days he was an amateur boxer and he seemed to have no fear. I remember the occasion when a man came into the office in a great temper threatening revenge; after he had been talking to Howard for some time he went out as mild as a lamb, repeating the solution which was really Howard's solution but which he thought was his own. Asked about it afterwards, Howard said; "Well, if anyone loses their temper I always feel that I can better them in the argument." He never let emotion interfere with his judgment; he just quietly knew what was the solution. During my working life of 60 years with him in the office he never lost his temper and I have a lasting admiration for him.

I remember the Dixon brothers calling in at the office in the morning and walking out together, the three of them, onto the lawn in front of the house, and if a telephone call came for them I went out to tell them. Colonel Dixon had a rolltop desk in our little office and he used to sit there and write away. Often he would get very hot because the fire was just behind his back and he called for me to come and put up a screen, which I did.

The Dixons were a wonderful family. Although tenants of the Hewell Estate, they were bosses in their own right. Each of the sons had his own house and four servants - cook, housemaid, gardener and chauffeur. Mr Ralph Dixon I admired very much indeed. He was a grand fatherly man who always considered other people and what was good for them.

Mr Hugh Dixon was always a great supporter of the Church and he was a warden there. Whilst he was churchwarden it was decided by the Parochial Church Council to hold a fete at Hewell Park to raise money to build a house at Webheath for the curate, and this turned into a very big affair. I was secretary of the poultry show which we held in the covered court at Hewell Grange. When arrangements for the staging fell through I went to see Mr Hugh Dixon and he fetched a farm lorry and together we went over to Dixons' Redditch timber yard, got the necessary staging, brought it back to Hewell and erected it.

The Dixon sons were all tall men, over 6 feet. Mr Ralph Dixon was a chartered accountant and he seemed to have endless mental energy and welcomed every opportunity that came along to extend the business. In addition to T & M Dixon Limited, the original family business which dealt in coal, he eventually established a garage at Redditch and depots around Birmingham, and at Harborne, Studley, Redditch and Bromsgrove. I have a note of the tonnage of the coal sold in the 12 months prior to March 1938 which amounted to 136 thousand tons, of which 65,593 tons 13 hundredweights were supplied to the Austin Motor Company at Longbridge to heat the factory. I remember that during the coal strike our directors were able to obtain brown coal from

Cannock Chase and our lorries collected it and delivered it to the factory. They were able to keep the factory going all through that period. The colliery bills used to come in monthly and I had the job of writing out the cheques for all these collieries. It impressed me, of course, being a young boy, to be able to draw cheques for very large amounts.

The farm business continued and Mr Ralph Dixon was particularly interested in poultry. He had the distinction of one of his hens winning the first national egg-laying competition in the country. I remember Mr Ralph decided to build a hundred new 30 ft poultry-laying sheds. He had worked out all the timber required and other items and he arranged for the carpenter and his assistants to make a model so that any of the people on the farm could come and help to slot the pieces of wood in the right position and nail the timbers. It was very interesting to see the automated sheds in operation. The number of poultry was increased, I think, to about 25,000 and they were all kept in open runs - free range. I remember that the exits for the birds were about 2 ft wide and we had a case of one of the local lads crawling into one of the pens and stealing the eggs, so we had to reduce the size of the hen exits. The eggs were crated and packed at Broad Green. They were packed in cartons holding 180 eggs and taken off to Birmingham either by lorry or by canal boat.

Dixons' motor boat *Enterprise* ran daily between Tardebigge and Birmingham carrying farm produce including eggs, milk and vegetables. At Birmingham the firm had a man with a horse and vehicle to deliver goods from the boat to the market. They used to load horse manure or whatever else there was to come back to Tardebigge on the boat. I remember we used to ring certain shops in Birmingham to order goods which had to be delivered to the Worcester Quay (at Gas Street Basin) for the boat to pick up. At times live pigs were taken in the boat to Birmingham and I remember one occasion when a sow got out of the boat on the way to Birmingham, about half way there I think, and escaped. Fortunately the local farmer looked after it and we were able to pick it up later.

On the farm they had 2,500 pigs and 160 cows and we used to deliver milk into Birmingham daily by boat to our depot at Harborne to a Mr Sherwood, who used to sell direct to private houses, and also to

Jack Houghton and, seated, Fred bird with the office cat in Dixons' Broad Green offices in 1947.

Birmingham General Hospital and the Erdington Hospital. On Sundays when the boat wasn't running one of the young men on the farm used to take a pony and a cart to travel all the way to Birmingham to deliver the milk to each hospital.

When Mr Best gave up Stoney Lane Farm, Mr Ralph Dixon was very interested to find he had been a fruit grower and from then on Mr Ralph took over and developed the fruit business until we could produce more than 100 tons each of strawberries, raspberries and blackcurrants in addition to a lot of plums. Then the growing of apples and pears extended until we had 50,000 fruit trees and, I think, about 2,000 tons of apples and pears to dispose of each year. For that purpose we had fruit stores erected at Broad Green to hold about 2,000 tons to enable the regulation of marketing to meet demand.

Mr A R MacDonnell came to Tardebigge as a pupil of Mr Ralph

Dixon and he lived at Stoney Lane House with Mr Ralph's family. He eventually married one of Mr Ralph's daughters, Honor, and later became a partner in Tardebigge Orchards. I can remember the board meeting at which he handed me his cheque for his share as a partner in the business.

I remember seeing Mr Ralph's son Peter as a baby in the pram and during his early years. When the Second World War started he joined the forces and was appointed a major in charge of an anti-tank battery. They were engaged in holding the Germans at the time the Americans were landing and Peter was awarded the Military Cross for his service. When the allies came to cross the Rhine in March 1945 Peter's battery of 400 men was to lead the crossing in gliders. His glider was shot down in flames with his crew. Mr Tipple, the father of our present church organist (at St Martin's, Worcester) was with Peter in the army. He should have been in Peter's glider but was moved at the last moment and observed Peter's glider falling in flames. Mr Tipple admired Peter because he showed great consideration for his men. Peter's commanding officer paid great tribute to him in the letter he wrote to his wife following his death.

The men who worked for the Dixons were a wonderful lot. Jim Jackson lived by the entrance to my orchard and he was extremely valuable to me because he was very experienced in tending the orchards, pruning and spraying.

George Knight was foreman in charge of the fruit growing. He came from Badsey, Evesham, and knew all there was to know about fruit growing. He was an excellent foreman and was well-liked. George had been brought up with womenfolk prejudiced against men going to the public house. However he regularly used to go off from the farm as he finished work and take short cuts across the fields down to Finstall where there was a small public house, The Cross. He was never drunk or anything like that, but we in the office used to know his whereabouts and watch him cross the fields on his way there.

The Colledge family lived at the New Wharf and were concerned with the boating. I remember the father; we used to see him from the office walking along the road on the way to Blackwell Station. He went up to Cannock to the colliery to supervise the loading of the boats because there was a lot of competition to get the boats loaded and Mr

Colledge senior was a proper foreman. He would regulate the loading. He used to boast that he could at times get extra coal because of the slope of the boat. I used to hear these stories but I was never quite convinced. I remember that when he was back at the New Wharf he used to fish out coal that had dropped into the canal when boats were being unloaded and use it.

The Dixons had a warehouse at the New Wharf beside the canal where they produced animal feeds from supplies of corn brought up by boat from Bristol. The power used was a big four-wheel portable steam engine which was used at The Lower House, a mile or more away, for threshing and other jobs on the farm. It was quite a major operation when the men had to move this steam engine from The Lower House to the New Wharf. They used to have some scotches which they would drop under the wheels to steady them when they were going downhill, otherwise it would have run into the horses.

When the foreman was away they sent me over to work at the wharf. We used to hoist the bags of corn from the canal to the upper floor of the warehouse, and then wheel them along and drop the contents into hoppers. One of these would kibble it - break it up - another one would crush the oats for horses, another would mix the ingredients. When using this third hopper on the top floor you had to come down, switch on the machine, and then pack the resulting animal feed into bags at the bottom. The horse corn was put into various lots for the different depots. We had to write out a ticket in the book: "Redditch, so many bags of chaff, horse corn for, say. 3 horses in so many bags". I had the job of entering up all the figures in the office and of charging the depots. We had to charge for the bags so that the depots would send them back, otherwise they might not have done so.

Sometimes Hugh Dixon would make a visit to the warehouse and go round it to see what was being done. He would then go out and you'd think 'Oh, he's gone' and you could take a breather. The funny thing was that he had a way of coming straight back in again.

The hours on the farm used to be 6.00 a.m. until 6.00 p.m., six days a week. Then they decided to allow the men to work two hours less on Saturday, finishing at 4.00 p.m. We thought that was grand. Later on John Bird, Howard's son, broke with tradition; he liked to go off sailing on Friday night and he gave the men Saturday off. That was a godsend

Peter Dixon

to me when I had my orchard.

When, after the second World War, the Plymouth estates were sold it was a calamity for Tardebigge and the farmers who were tenants of the Hewell estate because it covered such a large area including much of Redditch, Bromsgrove, and part of Birmingham, and it affected a lot of people. Four of the farmers concerned decided to form a syndicate to buy the estate so that they could offer each farmer a chance to buy his farm if he wanted to, and that's what they did. One of the four was my colleague and employer Mr Howard Bird, so that I was in touch with all that went on. When Howard was ill and in hospital I had to carry on in his place with the office work and keeping the accounts.

When they sold the estate there were some few farms left that were not cleared and a separate sale of these was held in Birmingham. On one of these farms was a small orchard of 20 acres in which I had always been interested because it was close to where I lived. I talked about it with my wife, but in those days I did not have the money to buy a farm just like that. However, my wife was a schoolteacher, a very capable person, and she went to the sale, bought the farm, rang me up on the telephone and said "I've bought that farm for £10,000". She deposited the £1,000 I'd given her. On the Monday morning I went to the office and, of course, they all knew about the sale and who had bought the farms. Howard was very kind to me. He arranged for me to buy my orchard for £750, so I had £250 back to provide the wherewithal to run it.

Tardebigge Orchards owned some 700 acres of farm land. They had 5,000 apple and pear trees and cold stores for 2,000 tons of fruit, which enabled us to regulate the marketing according to demand.

I have had an extraordinary life. Being in the office and as secretary you hear all the plans and are involved in carrying them out, which is all very interesting. In the end it came to me to see the end of the Plymouths at Tardebigge and the Dixons. When Howard died his son John accepted me almost in his father's place and we got on very well. He was a very thorough and successful farm manager and I greatly appreciated his kindness and friendship.

Chapter Four
Memories of Employees of T & M Dixon and Others

Over the years a great many people were employed by Dixons in various ways. Many worked on the farms, in charge of livestock or on the arable side in the growing of corn, fruit and vegetables, flowers, mushrooms etc. Besides the full-time farm workers there were many casual labourers, including children and people from near and far who helped with fruit-picking. Men were employed in the transport of coal,

Tom Colledge, in charge of T & M Dixon's fleet of canal boats.

timber, farm produce and other commodities on the roads and using the canals. The businesses in coal, timber, lime and building materials

The Governor (Matthew Dixon) riding in a trap with his groom George Smith.

provided work for other people. There were staff employed in offices and depots at Tardebigge, Redditch and elsewhere. In addition there were those employed in the various Dixon households as maids, cooks, nannies, chauffeurs and gardeners. The memories of many of these employees have provided an insight into the domestic and business activities of the Dixon family in more recent times.

EVELYN CARR was the second of eleven children of John and Emma Colledge who lived on Tardebigge New Wharf. Her father and her grandfather Thomas Colledge worked as boatmen for T & M Dixon. Evelyn was born in 1906 and on leaving Tardebigge School in 1921 she went to work as a domestic servant at The Lower House. At that time living there were old Matthew Dixon ('The Governor'), his daughters Grace and Jane and Jane's husband Dr Basil William Housman, together with a complement of servants which included the cook (an elderly lady), housemaid (Betty Fisher, one of Evelyn's cousins), parlour maid (Alice Evans, daughter of Dixons' shepherd John Evans) and kitchen maid (Evelyn). In addition there was a pony and trap driver, later chauffeur, George Smith, and a part-time gardener. Evelyn and the other domestic servants lived in, and, besides her keep. she was paid £16 a year by instalments at the end of each calendar month. As kitchen maid she had to be up by 6.30 a.m. to light the fire in the kitchen range. Matthew Dixon was by this time very old and for the last year or so of his life was an invalid looked after by Mrs Housman with the help of nurses. After Matthew's death in 1924 Dr and Mrs Housman managed with only two resident servants, a cook (Mabel Crowther from Stoke Prior) and a house parlour maid (Evelyn). Dr Housman died in 1932 and Evelyn continued to work at the Lower House until Mrs Housman died in 1937 and her sister Grace then went to live with Harvey Dixon at Tutnall.

Dr Housman, who worked as a medical officer for schools for Worcestershire County Council (he used to visit Tardebigge School) and as a TB doctor, was a brother of the poet A E Housman, then Professor of Latin at Trinity College, Cambridge, and of the writer Laurence Housman. Evelyn remembers visits of A E Housman to the Lower House to stay. He usually came for a week or a fortnight at a time. During his stay he did a lot of walking around the countryside, and on

Tardebigge Orchards apple trees in blossom below Tardebigge Church.

Sundays George Smith took him by car to Bromsgrove Parish Church for the morning service and he walked back. One of Evelyn's tasks was to take a large white enamel can of hot water to his bedroom for his morning ablutions at 7.00 a.m. She also waited at table. For each week of his holiday he used to give her half-a-crown. Laurence Housman also came to stay occasionally. He lived with his sister Clemence in Street, Somerset, and travelled up in his own car driven by his chauffeur Wilks.

Evelyn remembers the new offices at Broad Green being erected soon after the 1914-18 War. They had been in use as an army hospital in the London area and were of timber construction. The reconstruction was carried out by Rowland Smith, carpenter, whose wife Fanny ran the post office at 3 New Wharf, and Dan Fisher, builder, of Bromsgrove, both of whom were uncles of Evelyn. At about the same time they also built the two bungalows nearby facing the crossroads at Broad Green. Evelyn also recalls that before the Broad Green Offices were built she used to take her father John's wages bill for the hours he worked to Colonel Dixon's office at The Cottage.

PETER VOLLER is the youngest of the three children of Jack Voller and his first wife, Emily Louise, who died when Peter was only five years old. Jack had worked for the Duke of Wellington at Stratfield Saye, south of Reading, before moving to Tardebigge in 1921 to work for T & M Dixon as foreman poultryman. He was married at Tardebigge and, after living for a while in White Cottage in Hewell Lane close to the Old Wharf where his childen were born, he moved with his family to live in Yew Tree Cottage, Dusthouse Lane, Tutnall. The cottage has since been demolished, but the yew tree remains just beyond Curtis Close. Jack was in charge of Dixons' widespread poultry farms for some thirty years until about 1951 when they came to an end. He was then unhappily made redundant and died not long afterwards.

Peter went to Tardebigge School and sang in the church choir. After working in industry in Redditch for a short while he was glad to find work with his father on the poultry side in 1940. He served in the navy 1943-6 and then returned to this work. Following his marriage he lived in what was believed to be the oldest house in Tardebigge, a seventeenth century wattle and daub cottage in Tutnall which was destroyed when the A449 dual carriageway was constructed. During and following World War 2 the poultry business was gradually reduced and after it finished Peter spent three years, 1951-4, on the soft fruit side before becoming an employee of the East Worcestershire Waterworks and looking after the 700 ft deep boreholes and the pumping station near the Old Wharf.

There used to be poultry almost everywhere on Dixons' farms, in fields adjacent to the Old Wharf, around Dusthouse Farm and Horns Hall, at The Elbows, at Burcot, at Blackwell and elsewhere. Poultry workers included, besides Peter and his father, George Collins, Dan Mascall, Alf Warman (who lived in the Weighbridge House on the Old Wharf and had a stiff leg after an accident), Bill Skillern and Len Voller (Peter's uncle). Each had his area of poultry to care for with well over a thousand birds. These were free-range, mostly in fields surrounded by wire netting and containing poultry houses, each for about 120 birds. Work would begin at about 7.00 a.m. with the release of birds from the houses. They had to be fed, the houses cleaned, eggs collected and taken to Broad Green for testing, grading and packing, and, around dusk, the hen houses had to be closed for the night. Some of the poultry, chickens and cockerels were killed and dressed for the table in a shed at Broad Green. Poultry farming was a seven-days-a-week full-time job, but to Peter it was very satisfying. One real problem he remembers was caused by courting couples in their cars parked in the farm gateways who did not like being disturbed to allow farm carts into the fields.

For some time Peter worked in the incubator houses, brick buildings, at Tutnall Farm. The breeding season was January to March. Eggs were hatched out and the chicks were sexed by visiting Japanese students. Most cock chicks went to Bromsgrove Market. Hen chicks were reared on the farm. In the 1940s Crispian Dixon and his widowed mother and their housekeeper lived in Tutnall Farmhouse. One night in 1948 Crispian went missing. He had shot himself and his body was found in the incubator houses the following morning by Peter and Mr Allan MacDonell - not a pleasant memory. Crispian was the last of the Dixons in the farming business.

MRS DORIS WARNER was only a young girl when her father Thomas Evans came to work for Dixons in 1922 as a general stockman. He and his wife Florence and their children Tom, Florence and Doris were the tenants of one of two new bungalows newly erected at Broad Green on the sliproad facing the crossroads. Their neighbours in the other bungalow were Joe Williams, his wife and family; Joe was a general farm worker and the brother of Jim Williams fruit foreman for Dixons. As stockman Thomas Evans had to be at Stoney Lane Farm by 6.00 a.m. each morning to milk the cows with George Burton. Besides looking after the cattle, they also looked after sheep and pigs on the farms.

Whilst Doris was a pupil at Tardebigge School her parents were appointed caretakers at Dixons' Broad Green offices (her father still continuing as stockman) and the family moved from the bungalow nearby into living accommodation at the Tutnall end of the office building. The previous caretaker had been Mrs Houghton, Jack Houghton's mother. The office building was ex-army, purchased by Dixons after world War 1. It was of plywood construction and it was

Early 1950s group of men employed by Dixons on fruit farming. From left to right, top row: Jack Billingham, Christopher Davies (also tractor driver), Trevor Lacy (also on building maintenance), Alf Warman; bottom row: Bill Perry (also lorry driver), Jack Large (also tractor driver), Jim Williams (foreman for The Lower House fruit section), Allen Voller (also lorry driver). Their work included spraying, digging around and pruning the fruit trees. The photograph was taken in one of the orchards near The Elbows.

centrally heated. The living accomodation comprised kitchen, living room, sitting room and three bedrooms. The coal-fired central heating boiler was under Doris's bedroom and she used to worry that the plywood walls got really hot. The offices contained a long room with four desks, one each for Fred Bird, Charles Wall, Jack Houghton and one spare. There was a board room where the Dixon brothers, Colonel Matthew, Hugh and Ralph, and Howard Bird would meet most days, a dining room, a typist's room, a telephone room with an exchange linking the Dixon houses to each other and to the office and an outside line, an upstairs store room, and, under the stairs, a strong room with safe. Outside the offices Dixons had their own two petrol pumps.

On week-days Doris's mother Florence provided coffee at 11.00, lunch at 1.00 and tea at 4.00 o'clock in the dining room for the office staff; and when Doris arrived home from school she was usually expected to help with the washing up. On pheasant shooting days Florence put on a beaters' lunch which always included apple cobs (whole Bramley apples with sugar encased in pastry). In the soft fruit picking season she worked until late in the evening helping to pay the fruit pickers as they exchanged their tallies for cash. They were paid through two sash windows of the dining room; the pickers queued up outside on a wooden platform. When Ralph Dixon died he left Florence £75 in his will in appreciation of her services.

Doris's older sister Florence became nursemaid to Ralph Dixon's son Peter at Stoney Lane Farm, and when Peter became of school age she stayed on in service there. Doris started school at Tardebigge at the early age of three, taken by her then nine-year-old sister, and, after leaving Tardebigge School at the age of fourteen, she began working for Dixons at Broad Green, grading and packing eggs. She continued working in the egg shed from 1933 until 1947. At times Doris and her fellow workers dressed poultry, killed by her father, in a small shed near the egg shed. She also helped with the packing of mushrooms which were grown in another shed there and in a nearby field, Edgar King being in charge.

Five or six people worked in the egg shed. Eggs which were brought in from poultry houses and from the fields were first cleaned with damp cloths. They were then 'candled', that is they were held in front of an electric lamp (a candle in the old days) in a darkened corner and rejected if they were not clear. Clear eggs then rolled down a metal channel onto the rotating disc of a Brecknall, Munroe and Rogers grader which sorted out the eggs by weight into large, standard, medium, small and pullet sizes, which went into separate partitions. Graded eggs were packed into large wooden boxes containing 30 dozen or into cardboard cartons containing 15 dozen for wholesale distribution. Various quantities went to regular customers such as the Midland Eye Hospital, the Birmingham General Hospital, and Nicholls and Son (Birmingham Market). Eggs were also sold locally. People came from miles around for cracked eggs (sold at 18 for less than a shilling). Broken eggs put into 2 lb jam jars went to De Gray's bakery, and sometimes Crane's bakery, in Bromsgrove.

When Doris started work at the age of fourteen in 1933 she was paid

2d per hour (7/6 per week after stoppages); then at age 16 it rose to 3½d per hour, and from the age of 18 it remained at 5d per hour. The hours were 8 - 1 and 2 - 6 Monday to Friday and 8 - 12 on Saturday, a 49 hour week. When Doris eventually took on more responsibility, including being in charge and dealing with the paperwork, her extra reward was just a £5 bonus at Christmas. She gave up her job soon after her marriage in 1946. Her parents continued as caretakers at the offices until her mother died in 1951 and her father then went to live with Doris and her family.

One of Doris's memories is of the numerous beehives to be seen in Dixons' orchards. The beekeeper was Mr. Gerrard who lived in Pikes Pool Lane. Some of the honey was sold at the Broad Green Offices. There was a local Bee Keeping Society which used to meet on Saturday afternoons at the Broad Green Offices and for whom Doris's mother provided teas.

As a child KEN CLARKE lived with his parents Hubert and Gertrude Clarke for two years in the early 1920s in one of the two cottages on the west side of the Old Wharf at Tardebigge. Their neighbours in the other cottage nearer the Brockhill Lane canal bridge were Fred and Annie Davis, with their family, who kept the post office there from 1922 to 1936. Ken's maternal grandfather was George Knight who lived at Horns Hall and who had migrated from Badsey near Evesham many years earlier to become fruit foreman for Dixons. It was George who got his son-in-law Hubert a job with Dixons a year or two after his service in the 1914-18 War and helped him to become an expert in grafting and pruning fruit trees. When Ken was still young his family moved to a cottage (now known as The Cottage) in Dusthouse Lane, where they lived for many years. Ken went to Tardebigge School and sang in the Tardebigge Church choir, and on leaving school at the age of 14 worked for Dixons for a few months before finding other work.

Ken Clarke has some interesting memories from his early years in Tardebigge in the 1920s and 1930s between the wars. On the Old Wharf there were usually up to half-a-dozen horse-drawn boats tied up. Some of these brought in manure for the fields and pig-food (spent hops from Davenport's canalside brewery and food waste from Birmingham shops and markets). Others delivered coal from various collieries which

A 1930s photograph of a display of chips of soft fruit with, left to right, Joel Williams (foreman and brother of Joe Williams), Micky Mullins, Thomas King (fruit foreman).

was stacked neatly for 50 yards or so along the side of the wharf. Some of the coal was sold directly to customers on the wharf for £1 per ton; some was delivered locally by horse and cart to agents or householders by Ted Laight or Harry Sumner. Two-wheel carts were used so that the coal could easily be tipped off. At the top end of the wharf opposite to the winding hole (known to the locals as the whirlpool) was the piggery. Pigs were housed in pens on both sides of a passage running the length of the ground floor of a two-storied wooden building about fifty yards long. Along the first floor above the passage ran the rails of a narrow gauge tramway. Pig food stored in a large container at the canal end of the building was conveyed in waggons along the track and tipped down chutes into the feeding troughs below. The butcher was Len Banner. The primitive slaughterhouse was one of the two old disused limekilns near the winding hole. Pigs were killed by having their throats slit and were then hoisted and dropped into a metal trough of boiling water heated by a fire below to loosen the bristles. Len sold pork on the wharf; purchasers were given the bill and paid it at Dixons' Broad Green offices.

Living in the next cottage in Dusthouse Lane to the Clarkes was Bill Marshall, his wife and family. At the back of the Marshalls' cottage there was an aviary in which were bred pheasant chicks. Of these some were let loose in the nearby Dusthouse quarry which at the time was a rough woodland area, others in the cutting south of Shortwood canal tunnel. When Bill Marshall moved to Grimley Cottage near to the canal his aviary was in a field nearby. Mainly on Saturdays the Dixons would invite the local gentry to a pheasant shoot held on their farmland. Ken Clarke remembers as a lad being employed as a 'stop' on the boundary of Dixon territory preventing birds from going off their land; or else acting as a beater, to cause the birds to rise into the air for the shoot. For this he and other farm workers were paid half-a-crown for some six to eight hours effort.

Another of Ken Clarke's memories is going strawberry picking before school with other children. They would start as soon as it was daylight, around 4.30 a.m. before the birds attacked the fruit. Often there was a heavy dew and their feet would get soaking wet. Another source of income derived from the problem of the rats on the farms, especially around the hen houses and piggeries; moles too in places. Youngsters could earn welcome pocket money by taking the tails of dead rats or moles to the Broad Green offices. They were paid two old pence for each one handed over.

HARRY SUMNER, born at Redhill near Alcester in 1895, left school at 11, as was usual in those days, and worked with horses on a farm at Binton. In 1923, following World War 1 in which he was wounded in France and underwent 23 operations, he went to work as waggoner for Dixons. With his wife Elizabeth and four children he lived in the weighbridge house on the Old Wharf and his job was to look after the 10 to 12 farm horses which were stabled at The Lower House and did most of the heavy work including haulage and ploughing. He had to be at the Lower House at 5.30 a.m. to take a horse to the Old Wharf by 6.00 a.m. ready for pulling one of Dixons' two boats, *Snowdrop* and *Albert Edward*, which in the 1920s and 1930s brought manure from Birmingham or coal from Cannock, a two-day trip. On occasions when the canal was frozen over, the whole team of 10 or more horses was used to pull the canal company's ice-breaking boat.

T. & M. DIXON LTD.

Coal and Timber Merchants and Garage Proprietors

MANUFACTURERS OF Portable Buildings, Poultry Appliances including Laying Houses (Patent Front), Brooder Houses, Brooders, Slatted Floor and Fold Houses, Wagon Scantlings, Coffin Boards (Oak and Elm), Fencing and Fencing Materials, Barrows, Ladders, Gates, Gate Posts, Line Props

All sizes
ENGLISH TIMBER
cut to order

COAL, COKE AND FIREWOOD
supplied at lowest prices

SAW MILLS
HEWELL ROAD
REDDITCH

Telephone
3 and 4

Advertisement in Redditch Official Guide 1933 for Dixons' timber business, cut timber, wooden buildings and other items of timber construction.

78

This advertisement in Redditch Official Guide 1947 gives some indication of the comprehensive nature of Dixons' non-farming business following World War 2.

Dixons' Hewell Road Garage

RAY KING began working in 1946 for T & M Dixon and then continued to work for Tardebigge Orchards and subsequently for John Bird who continues to manage Lower House Farm and Dusthouse Farm. Ray's grandfather Thomas King and his wife Martha came to Tardebigge in the 1890s from Hereford via Rushock to work for Dixons on the soft fruit side. They lived in one of the three Stoney Lane Cottages created by dividing up what had been a farmhouse. Eventually Thomas became a soft fruit foreman. They had ten children. One, Edgar, worked for Dixons and took over as a soft fruit foreman when his father died in 1941. Another, Amy, married Jim Williams who was also a soft fruit foreman for Dixons and later looked after the apple trees of Tardebigge Orchards.

JANET ARCHER, a cousin of Ray King, also has memories of her grandfather Thomas King and her uncle Edgar. Janet's husband Fred worked in Dixons' office at Broad Green with Jack Houghton and Fred Bird (a cousin of Howard Bird), and he was also employed at the timber and coal office at Hewell Road Wharf, Redditch.

FRED SKILLERN was a transport driver for Dixons for many years. He started work in 1937 after leaving Tardebigge School at the age of 14, and from 1948 to 1973 he drove an 'artic' (articulated lorry) deliverying soft fruit countrywide. He needed nerves of steel to draw two trailers as far as London, Southampton, Liverpool and Dundee - this was before the bringing in of restrictions on the working conditions of HGV drivers.

Fred's grandfather George Skillern came to Tardebigge with his wife Sarah from Severn Stoke around 1894 when Dixons advertised widely for farm workers. They lived in one of the three Stoney Lane Cottages into which, as already mentioned, an old farmhouse had been

One of Dixons' lorries in a carnival procession in Redditch

converted. George looked after the cart horses, pairs being used for ploughing, and also the horses ridden by various members of the Dixon family. George's son Matthew, Fred's father, married Lizzie Gertrude Jones, and they also lived in Stoney Lane Cottages before moving to the Old Wharf in 1929 with their two young children Nancy and Fred. In the 1920s and 1930s Matthew drove a Sentinel steam lorry and petrol lorries for Dixons. One of his jobs was to fetch and return, by lorry, soft-fruit pickers who came for the day to Tardebigge from Brierley Hill in the season. He also fetched those soft-fruit pickers from the Black Country, mainly women and their children, who came to stay in the barns at Dusthouse and Lower House farms or in a wooden building at Horns Hall for several weeks in the Summer. Their trunks and belongings were piled into the lorry and they sat on top. It was for them a working holiday.

Fred and his sister Nancy went to Tardebigge School. He sang in the church choir, pumped the organ before the blower was electrified, and was a server. Nancy remembers walking each Sunday over the Shaws to church and back from the Old Wharf to Sunday School at 10.15 a.m.

Arthur Cole with one of Dixons' Austin vans.

followed by Mattins, and then again in the evening to Evensong at 6.30 p.m. Fred remembers having a ride on Dixons' motor boat *Enterprise* in 1929 at the age of six when his maternal grandfather Ernest Jones was its skipper. He also remembers some old rails from the railroad that used to run from Dusthouse Quarry up to the Canal below the top lock being unearthed at the quarry end. In 1972/3 when Tardebigge Orchards, besides doing away with the orchards and soft-fruit growing, sold the Dusthouse Farmhouse and many cottages, the tenants, many of whom had been employees of T & M Dixon, had to find other homes, and this included Fred Skillern and his wife who moved to Stoke Prior.

Fred's wife Joyce was one of the two daughters of William Perry who, like Fred's father Matthew, drove a petrol lorry for Dixons between the Wars. William and his wife and family lived in one of the two cottages into which Horns Hall had been divided before they moved into a cottage in Hewell Lane near The Elbows. Following World War 2 William continued to drive a petrol lorry to take farm produce into Birmingham and he also drove tractors on the farms, continuing for a time under Tardebigge Orchards. Joyce worked at times for Dixons, check-weighing fruit at Broad Green packing shed (twenty or so people worked there in season) under the foreman Ray King.

Information about Dixon's use of canal transport has been supplied by three of JOHN COLLEDGE'S SONS, TOM, FRANK and WILFRED. Tom and Frank at times worked with their father as well as with others on Dixons' boats. In the 1920s Tom assisted his father and then from 1928 to 1934 worked on his own account for Dixons with, as mate, his elder brother John Henry or his father. Their horse-drawn boats did two trips each week fetching coal from Cannock or Polesworth. They also brought limestone from Dunhampstead to Tardebigge, market waste and manure from Birmingham and spent hops from Davenport's canalside brewery. They mostly went empty to Birmingham, but sometimes carried hay to Worcester Wharf at Gas Street Basin. The waste from Birmingham went to provide bedding and food for the many pigs kept at the Old Wharf. Brothers Frank and Len Banner loaded it onto trucks on a 2 ft gauge tramway which ran from the canalside into the piggery. By this time (1930s) one of the old lime kilns had become the pig slaughter-house, Len Banner being the butcher, and pig meat was sold on the wharf. Frank remembered his grandfather Tom Colledge who, in the late 1800s had been in charge of a fleet of 50 or so Dixon boats and the boatmen, including providing these men

with food. Grannie Colledge (née Mary Walton) fed the boatmen
spotted dick made in a canvas sleeve so that they did not need so much
meat. Frank's father John had been injured as a baby; he wore a surgical
boot because one leg was shorter than the other, but he was quite agile.
He would not tolerate bad language and he neither smoked nor drank.
He considered himself a cut above other canal boatmen. He was a good
Christian and taught 'no revenge'.

Frank Colledge accompanied his father John on Dixons' horsedrawn
boats *Snowdrop* and *Albert Edward* for about twelve months in the early
1930s when jobs were in short supply. Both boats had a sparsely-
equipped cabin with no mattress or bedding and the crew slept on old
coats. Each trip to fetch up to 33 tons of coal from Cannock took two
days and on arrival the coal had to be neatly stacked on the Old Wharf
beside the canal.

JIM BURTON as a child lived in one of the Stoney Lane Cottages
near Harris's Bridge over the canal. His father George and his uncle Bill
worked as stockmen for Dixons. The family came from Stoke Prior
where Jim's grandfather was employed at the salt works and George
was the eldest of nineteen children. George obtained work in
Wolverhampton as the driver of a horse tram. One day he parked his
tram outside a pub and whilst he was inside the horse walked away
with the tram and George got the sack. Fortunately Bill who was
already working as a cowman for Dixons was able to get his brother
George a similar job.

Jim was born in Wolverhampton and moved with his parents to
Tardebigge at the age of three. On leaving Tardebigge School he worked
for Dixons for a short time before spending most of his working life at
the Austin Works, Longbridge. He remembers his mother Mary
working as a V.A.D. nurse during the First World War at the Tardebigge
Village Hall which was turned into a hospital for wounded soldiers.
Like many other local children Jim learnt to swim in the canal at
Harris's Bridge; this location was known as "The Bather" and was
popular with Royal Enfield workers who came from Redditch via
Brockhill Lane to wash in the canal. Milk in churns from Stoney Lane
Farm was loaded into Dixons' motor boat *Enterprise* at 7.00 a.m. each
morning by the bridge. At the Old Wharf brothers Sam and Len Banner

and also Tommy Carter dealt with the coal sales, using the weighbridge which used to be there in front of the weighbridge house, and they also looked after the piggery there. Jim was one of many children who enjoyed rides on the canal tug with Charlie Hawkins and John Colledge through Tardebigge and Shortwood Tunnels and along the canal in between.

During World War 2 secondary school children from Wiltshire and elsewhere came to stay as fruit pickers. A letter received from JOHN MACDONALD in 1993 describes his own visit with a school party from Euclid Street Grammar School, Swindon, in the early 1940s:

Our school were invited to pick raspberries and blackcurrants in your parish because farm labourers were short due to the war. We came by train to Bromsgrove Station, cycled to Tardebigge, filled our palliasses with straw and were then allocated sleeping quarters in a huge barn not far from the canal where many of us learnt to swim. Some of the older boys said they had swum through a long tunnel but I did not witness it.

It never rained in those days. Staff helped supervise the fruit picking, making sure we did not miss any. We were given tallies after our 'weigh-in' at the end of the day. Cups of tea and large slices of slab cake were much appreciated, as was the food back at the camp.

Our latrines were a work of art and brought us close together as you might expect sitting at a 'four-holer'. Showers were also available at the end of a hot sticky day in the fruit fields.

We have fond memories of local farm supervisors. I can still recall Bill and Jim who had a fine Brummie dialect.

The farm where the school party stayed was Dusthouse Farm; the tunnel through which some boys claimed to have swam was Tardebigge Tunnel between the Old and New Wharves; and the farm supervisors were the fruit foremen Bill Clinton and Jim Williams. Many children learnt to swim and used to swim in the canal until after World War 2, and swimming through a tunnel was a feat to boast about. Amongst other children who came from Swindon to pick fruit was Diana Dors who was later well known as an actress.

JOHN BIRD, son of Howard Bird, started working for T & M Dixon (Farmers) in 1937. He remembers that at that time, just before World War 2, there were no tractors on the farms; all the heavy work being

Harry Thompson(left of group) with employees at T & M Dixon's garage in 1975.

done by horses. The livestock included about 180 milking cows at the Lower House, George Burton being the head cowman there. There were some 3,000 pigs located at the Old Wharf, Burcot Farm and Ashborough's Farm; 800 sheep; and 49,000 free range hens scattered around the farms. Large quantities of eggs were delivered to Cadburys, Bournville, for the making of Bournvita. Much of the farmland was given over to soft fruit, there being about 130 acres of strawberries, 120 acres of raspberries, 100 acres of blackcurrants, 13 acres of loganberries and blackberries, and 12 acres of redcurrants. Cadburys took delivery of quantities of soft fruit for the real fruit fillings of their chocolates. There were also about 80 acres of apple orchards both cookers and dessert, 80 acres of dessert pears and 120 acres of plums. Most of the plums went to Beeches of Evesham for jam making, and the surplus to Sona canners at Stratford-upon-Avon.

Other items of information gleaned from John Bird include his understanding that T & M Dixon were the first people in England to bottle milk which they supplied to hospitals in Birmingham, instead of using churns, and to have a milking machine; they were the first people to have a Massey-Harris combine harvester which was drawn by a 69 HP Buick petrol-driven vehicle; that Ralph Dixon initiated the practice of painting white lines on roads when, without permission, he painted a white line in the middle of the road on the dangerous bend in the old Bromsgrove to Redditch Road at Tutnall in the 1930s to prevent accidents there; and that he had seen a written agreement between T & M Dixon and the LMS Railway Company giving Dixons the right to use a railway crossing, accessed by side lanes to Hewell Lane at Vigo to take high-loaded vehicles such as hay carts over the Lickey railway incline if they were too tall to pass under the railway bridge there.

JOHN SMITH, when young, lived in Hewell Road, Redditch, not far from to the gates of T & M Dixon's coal wharf and timberyard. He remembers in 1928 at the age of eight playing in the yard with Harvey Hope, then aged thirteen, the son of Mr Hope the yard caretaker. At that time there were two gated entrances to the yard with, between them, a weighbridge, two terraced houses, the first of which was the caretaker's house, and a small garage with, at the side, petrol pumps. The price of a gallon of petrol was then 1s 1/2d (just over 5p) and the brand was R.O.P. (Russian Oil Products). When Dixons became agents for Austin cars, the garage was greatly enlarged with showrooms fronting onto Hewell Road and extensive repair and body and fitting shops behind. About 1950 T & M Dixon Ltd opened their subsidiary garage in Easemore Road where now is the Social Services building; it sold petrol and oil and carried out mechanical repairs.

Through the main gates to Dixons, yard on the lefthand side was their timberyard. Here a large area was occupied by a stack of tree trunks which were brought in by road and lifted and moved by a huge travelling crane the traverser of which moved on two sets of rails about 50 yards long mounted on girders some seventy feet above the ground and about 40 yards apart. The crane operator sat in a little cabin which moved with the crane high above ground and one of his jobs was to move logs onto a rolling deck which conveyed them to the circular saw benches to be sawn into planks of various thicknesses. The sawn timber was stacked for six months or more for seasoning in the open air with spacers between the planks to allow the air to circulate. Harvey Hope spent a lot of his time climbing over the stack of tree trunks and up into the crane girders rather like a human monkey. John Smith remembered the great fire of 1925 which burnt out the sawmill and seeing great chunks of blazing debris floating in the air over a wide area and firemen working through the night to quell the fire. The sawmill was soon rebuilt and other damage repaired and the timber business continued until around 1960.

In the 1920s logs from the Hewell Estate were transported to the timberyard by Dixons' own steam traction engine driven by Clem Halling. The sight of this great black monster, with smoke and sparks shooting from its chimney and its great flywheel spinning round, hauling two trailers, one loaded with huge tree trunks and the second with the tackle and smaller logs, along the country roads from Brockhill Woods and other areas of woodland, was very impressive, much more so than the diesel tractor which later replaced it. The steam traction engine had a piercing steam whistle and a man who walked fifty yards ahead of it to warn oncoming traffic of its approach along the narrow winding Brockhill Lane.

Besides dealing in coal and timber at the yard, Dixons also sold from there hay, farm feed of various kinds, paving slabs, fencing and building materials. bags of lime, fertilisers, peat, sand and farm manure. There were covered areas where some of these items were stored.

ARTHUR COLE worked as chief mechanic at Dixons' Hewell Road Garage for 50 years from 1929 to 1978, He had attended Tardebigge School from 1916 to 1925 under Mr Dilkes. His father had a farm at Upper Shortwood just beyond the house where Ernald Dixon lived and he knew Colonel Dixon. Arthur started working as mechanic for Dixons when Ernald Dixon was secretary; he continued under Howard Bird and later Bill Thompson, and for the last six years he worked for Roger Hill who took over Dixons' business in 1972, still trading as T &

M Dixon. The manager of the garage for many years was Frank Allwood; he was in charge of the sales from the start of the car retail business and he lived with his wife in Hewell Road in the double-fronted house (still standing) between the garage and the railway bridge. When Arthur started work the garage was used solely to service T & M Dixons' own vehicles; they then had about 15 of their own small lorries, five of them being steam lorries (3 sentinels and 2 yorkshires). The steam lorries finished a few years before World War 2. Arthur's job in the early days was simply to service Dixons' vehicles at the garage or at the directors' houses and also the electric generators. The agency for Austin cars began in 1925 and it continued until the garage closed.

DORIS EVANS worked in Dixons' Hewell Road, Redditch, offices from 1943 to 1972. In 1943 the directors of the coal business were Howard Bird, Allan McDonnell and Owen Goodrick-Clark. The general manager of the coal business had been Benjamin Huntley who lived at Barnt Green. His successor as transport manager for coal was Norman Cook. Doris started as office junior under Norman Cook and went on to become Company Accountant. After British Anthracite bought T & M Dixon's coal business, Doris was employed in their garage business and in the end became accountant for Graham Hill and Sons of Studley when they took over the Hewell Road Garage. She has been most helpful in providing details of the final years of Dixons' business operations in Redditch.

MATTHEW DIXON, son of Ralph Dixon and the elder brother of Crispian and Peter Dixon, left Malvern College in 1928 and worked for a short time in Dixons' offices, including their Birmingham office. At that time the various Dixon households were connected by telephone with each other and to the outside world via their own telephone exchange at the Broad Green office, the telephone number of which was Bromsgrove 7. Matthew soon decided that farming was a hazardous enterprise in which he was not really interested.

He studied architecture, then spent six years serving in the army during World War 2. In 1949 he and two other partners each invested £3,000 in buying a thatched public house, *The Black Horse*, together with three cottages, at Shipston-on-Stour in the Totswolds. The public house was restored and run for two years before being sold. Since that time Matthew has lived in London, a self-confessed 'rolling stone', having engaged in a series of business ventures including the manufacture of shirts and a laundry.

Hugh Dixon in 1907

I had almost despaired of finding a photograph of Hugh Dixon until, as this book was nearing completion, Matthew found he had one together with that of the four other sons of Matthew Dixon mounted in a souvenir presented to their father and mother on the occasion of their Golden Wedding in 1907 by Canon Dickens, Vicar of Tardebigge. It is strange, but perhaps typical of the times, that the five daughters of 'The Governor' were not included in this souvenir.